Secretes of Manipulation, Persuasion and Suggestion

Learn How to Influence People and Gain Their Trust, Improve Your Confidence and Become Master of Your Own Mind

ADAM HOOK

ISBN: 9781-6-925-8412-2

Secretes of Manipulation, Persuasion and Suggestion

CONTENTS

INTRODUCTION

Manipulation takes on various forms in everyday life, sometimes without people knowing it is occurring. Manipulation can be defined as a tool that is used to control and or influence a person or thing, in order to benefit oneself in some way. The individual being manipulated often is unaware it is happening. Manipulation can be found in all forms of relationships, in the workplace, and at home.

The way in which manipulation operates is it uses emotions, behavior, and relationships to alter perceptions of a particular situation or another person. Speech, actions, and situations are common forms of how a manipulative person can alter perceptions. There is a multitude of reasons for why individuals manipulated; some of the main reasons for why people do so are a need for power and control, to get some type of personal gain, if the person has low self-esteem, and if the individual is bored.

The manipulator and the manipulated have separate characteristics that either make it easy to trick others or make it easier to be tricked. Some of the types of people who tend to be manipulators are narcissists, sociopaths, psychopaths, abusers. These individuals believe their wants and needs are more important than the wants and needs of the people around them. Manipulators are often unaware or dismissive of boundaries of other people. The manipulator will pry and exploit whatever they can about another person, with no concern for the person being manipulated. In relation to exploiting others, the manipulator typically is unable to accept responsibility for what can come as a result of their actions. Additionally, the way in which manipulators are able to misuse the people around them is through their ability to observe the people around them to find their weaknesses.

The people who are more susceptible to having their weaknesses used against them are children and teenagers, optimists, and individuals who have had a traumatic experience in the past. The common traits of people who are manipulated easily include an abnormally strong need to please others, being naïve or immature, being emotionally dependent on other people, having a difficult time being assertive, and are intimidated by confrontation. These individuals also tend to have a tough time telling other people "no", which means they are more likely to go along with whatever is asked of them.

Even though the statements above are viewed as being negative, there can be instances where manipulation can be a positive action and beneficial to both the manipulator *and* the manipulated. One everyday occurrence of manipulation that is valuable to both parties is marketing. For example, with the knowledge of the effects of smoking tobacco, commercials have been created to try and prevent smoking. The main goal of the commercials is to evoke an emotional response of fear and discomfort to the viewers. As a result, this form of manipulation is aiming to protect the lives of the viewers. Another example takes place at home. When kids are younger, some parents embrace the word "can't". If a parent says to their child, "can you get into bed" a typical child will respond with "no". However, if a parent challenges their child with, "I bet you can't get into bed by yourself" the child more often than not jump into bed to prove their parent wrong. When the word manipulation is used, a negative connotation is automatically partnered with it; however, there can be cases where manipulation can be used to benefit both the manipulator and the person being manipulated.

The information that will follow contains a deeper understanding of the tools that are used to manipulate and persuade other people. It is necessary to learn the manipulation techniques because once an individual is aware of the methods; they can stop themselves from falling prey to a manipulator. A clear understanding of the manipulation techniques can also aide a person who has intentions of using manipulation to positively assist someone else.

WHAT IS MANIPULATION AND HOW IT WORKS

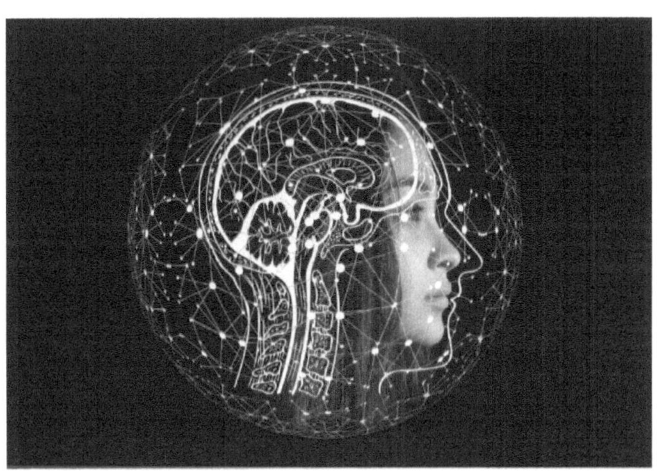

In order to recognize how manipulation works, it is important to understand the mechanisms of the human mind. The unconscious mind makes up almost all of the brain's functions. It controls your breathing, digestion, heart rate, etc. It is home to your creativity and imagination, and memories. It is also used to build your automatic response to feeling threatened. Your emotions are also present in the unconscious mind. Manipulative people play largely on the unconscious mind by altering another person's emotional response to someone. An individual who is a successful manipulator can make others feel comfortable and calm while covertly getting people to do what *they* want.

Manipulation is made possible through the use of psychology. Manipulators use psychological tactics to give an individual a false sense of security which then leads to the level of trust that the manipulator is seeking. It is when the manipulator gains another person's trust that the true mind games begin.

The psychology behind manipulation focuses on the idea that instead of making someone do what you want them to do, it is the key to make another person *want* to do what you want them to do. The way in which a manipulator is able to make this happen is through understanding the person they are trying to manipulate. The genuine wants and desires of the person being manipulated must be learned so that the manipulator can modify said wants and desires to match their own goals. The most important thing a manipulator should keep in mind is that the closer they are to the person being manipulated, the easier it will be to manipulate them. It takes time and patience to build this level of trust and the top manipulators take the time to learn the best way to manipulate a certain person at a particular moment.

One of the most common forms of manipulation comes in the form of emotional and psychological manipulation. Psychological manipulation focuses on the unevenness of power between people. The individual with the power preys on the weaknesses of the other person. The cycle of this form of manipulation is the manipulator finds an individual's weaknesses, the manipulator takes advantage of said weaknesses, and then the process continues to repeat. Once a manipulator successfully manipulates a person, they are not likely to stop manipulating until being forced to stop.

While it can be difficult to take notice of when one is being manipulated and stop someone from manipulating, there are ways to protect one's mind from manipulation. One tool that can be helpful is meditation. When a person is able to silence their mind and become more grounded, it can be noticeably easier to deal with emotional and psychological manipulation. Even when other people are hostile and controlling, an individual with inner peace can remain calm but aware of the manipulator's intentions. Avoiding an emotional attachment to manipulative people is also crucial. This approach can be challenging, especially if the manipulator is showing false signs of kindness to gain a person's trust. The best way to weed out the manipulators is to pay attention to any of the beginning signs that someone is overpowering someone emotionally. Once there is any warning of emotional manipulation, it is time to slowly back out of the relationship before attachment forms.

A manipulative person strives for power over another person. And so, by not allowing the manipulator into one's head, the manipulator loses their power. An individual can prevent a manipulator from getting into their head by laughing at their insults or statements and going along with what they say without actually agreeing with what is said. It is also extremely important to focus on one's own idea of self rather than how others see them. When a person has a solid sense of self-worth, it becomes nearly impossible for others to weaken that self-assurance. One finally a tool that can be used to stop manipulation is escaping from harmful relationships. People cannot be forced to change, it is best to save oneself from toxic relationships before the physical and emotional threat becomes too dangerous. Every person deserves to be in relationships where they are valued rather than ones that break a person down.

In order to prevent manipulation, one must first become aware of the signs of manipulation. One of the most common red flags that manipulation is taking place is if an individual is feeling guilty. Manipulators thrive on making the people around them feel bad about themselves. Since manipulators are unable to own up to their own faults, they tend to place blame onto other people, which thus creates guilt for the person being manipulated. This is commonly known in abusive relationships when the abuser says that it was the victim who made them act in an aggressive way. The victim of a manipulator will truly believe that it is their fault and stay in the toxic relationship. A manipulator will also use the controlled person's words against them to gain power and enforce the guilt approach. In relation to this tactic, manipulators are also able to plant their own ideas into other people's head. This is done by making assumptions about ideas that mirror their own desires. The manipulator is also skilled at making it appear that conflict has already been resolved when in actuality it has not. This can benefit the controlling individual because it ensures that the manipulator gets their way without having to confront any of their faults. A manipulative person also has the ability to not say anything to get what they want. The "silent treatment" is a useful tool to get into a person's head because the manipulator has already established a power position. In turn, the person being controlled will feel forced to give in to what the manipulator wants.

Once all of the signs of manipulative behavior have been comprehended, it then becomes important to understand the power of emotion in connection to manipulation. An individual's emotions play a vital role in one's ability to manipulate and to be manipulated. Emotion is one of the main tools used in manipulation. Manipulators will use an emotional connection to get as much information from another person as possible. This is also the main outlet of learning the weaknesses of the individual being manipulated. Additionally, manipulators will fake emotion at times in order to strategically undermine a person's decisions and create a level of self-consciousness. If a person's sudden onset of emotion does not appear genuine, call them out or get out of the relationship.

Sometimes it may take time for an individual to pick up on the warning signs of manipulation. However, one can train the brain to take notice of seemly innocent words and actions that can lead to manipulation. It may seem flattering if a partner wants to know what the other person is up to. However, when a boyfriend or girlfriend is constantly asking what the other person is doing and becomes angry when they do not receive an answer, this should send off a warning sign in the head. This can be an indication that the partner is monitoring their significant other and can even go as far as to turn into stalking.

People with a narcissistic personality tend to have the absence of object constancy which means their affection for a person evaporates when they become angry. This can become apparent because of what the narcissistic person may say when they become enraged. When this occurs, it appears as though the manipulator is a completely different person. If someone is being manipulated and this type of situation occurs, one can train the mind to pick up on the words being used that show a lack of connection between two people.

Manipulators will also not only place blame onto others but accuse others of doing exactly what the manipulator has done. For example, a manipulator would claim their partner must be cheating on them, but they are in fact the one who has cheated. If an individual looks back at some of the conversations they have had with a manipulator, they may learn more about the true actions of the said manipulator.

A question that is often wondered by people who hear of someone having been in an abusive relationship is *how could they have stayed with the person?* An abuser manipulates their partner into staying by providing moments of love. The abuser attempts to reel their partner in again after moments of violence by providing compliments or gifts. It is important for the brain to recognize that this does not mean the abuse will stop; it is only a ploy to make the person stay. Get out of the relationship as quickly as possible.

Abusers are also aware that many people draw the line at physical abuse. It can be more difficult to detect psychological abuse. However, there are still ways to train the mind to pick up on psychological trauma. Conversations surrounding jealousy can be a great indicator. If a partner is constantly jealous of their significant other spending time with other people, they are most likely trying to isolate their victim from everyone else. The manipulator is attempting to create a false notion that the partner can only rely on the manipulator.

Once an individual is able to train the mind to pick up on manipulative tendencies and phrases, it is time to get out of a manipulative situation altogether. The way an individual responds to manipulation depends on the type of manipulation that is taking place. If a person finds them self in a situation where the manipulator is aggressive, for example, an abusive relationship, it is wise to speak with a professional about the best way to exit. Speaking to a therapist or a hotline that specializes in domestic violence are two great tools to find the safest course of action.

If an individual is being manipulated but does not feel a sense of danger, either physically or emotionally, it becomes important to not allow the manipulator's words to sink in, let it go in one ear and out of the other. It is also strategic to create boundaries. Manipulators tend to create boundaries that are far too strict or too involved. It is helpful if the manipulated person responds by following their own boundaries and disregarding the manipulators. One last response to manipulation is to not make any rash decisions. Do not sign a contract or agree to any major decisions without truly thinking it over on one's own. This allows for the person to rationally come to a conclusion without a manipulator's own desires being the focal point.

Another approach to preventing or stopping oneself from being manipulated is to rewire the brain to be socially dominant. Studies have shown that social dominance is not improved by heightening the level of aggression or physical strength a person is exerting. Instead, when an individual becomes more resilient, dominance can be achieved. When a person is able to find success in one area of their life, they can translate that mindset into other instances of their life. Additionally, attempting to transform oneself into an extrovert can be useful. Extroverts tend to exhibit high levels of social dominance. To become an extrovert, an individual must be open-minded. Some of the traits of an extrovert are perceived as negative, but focusing on the positive attributes can help a person develop some of the desirable character traits of an extrovert. Another way to look at extroverts in a positive light is to think of influential people who are considered extroverts.

The next step is to practice the behaviors of an extrovert until they become natural. Specifically, look at opportunities to call attention to oneself is a beneficial way to learn to interact with all types of people. However, if an individual truly cannot be an extrovert, it is still possible to act the part. Plenty of famous actors pretend to be an extrovert on screen but are actually introverts behind the scenes. One example is Johnny Depp. The Hollywood star has played the roles of extroverts such as Willy Wonka and Captain Jack Sparrow, but in real life, Depp chooses to stay away from social situations.

Learning from others is another possible way

to become an extrovert. There tends to be more than one personality type in a given group of people, including extroverts. Watch how the extroverts in the group act compared to oneself and replicate their behavior. One final option is to have a complete understanding of oneself. What makes one person different from another person? Once an individual knows who they are, they can begin to look at how they are perceived by the people around them. This leads to a person's ability to see what attributes they have that other people respond to in a positive way and which characters can still be improved upon. The extrovert is not as easily manipulated, which promotes the act of transforming, even if it only on the surface, into an extrovert.

PERSUASION AND PERSUASION TECHNIQUES

There is a fine line between persuasion and manipulation, so fine that the line almost seems to disappear. Persuasion is when an individual is able to influence another person into believing something. There is a level of self-interest with persuasion and the aim is to change the viewpoint of one individual to match that of another. While on the surface, persuasion and manipulation appear to be the exact same, there is a distinct difference between the two. Persuasion allows for an individual to hear the truth about a matter and come to their conclusion about whether or not to change their own viewpoint. For example, if one person attempts to prove to another person that a particular type of phone is better than another phone, they will describe the phone's best features in the hopes that those said features are more desirable than the other phone's features.

Dissimilarly, manipulation uses coercion to trick another person into believing something without their knowledge that the trickery is taking place. For example, if one person is speaking about a product as though it is obvious that the product should be viewed in a negative light, this may force another person to unintentionally view the product negatively as well.

Persuasion uses its own techniques separate from manipulation to influence other people. One option is the foot in the door tactic which states that an individual asks for a small favor that leads to the asking of larger requests. By starting out with a smaller favor, an individual is promising to help someone else. Once the larger request is asked, it acts as a continuation of the initial smaller request. An example of this action would be if a person started out asking "Would you mind babysitting my kids tonight?" and then moving up to "Watch my kids for a couple of days; I'm going on a little trip." An experiment was conducted in the '60s to analyze the effectiveness of the foot in the door technique. Women were divided into four groups. Three of the groups were first asked questions about their kitchen appliances in their homes. Later on, the same three groups were asked if the researchers could directly go into the kitchens and record each individual kitchen appliance. The fourth group of women was only asked the second round of more evasive questions. The results showed that the women who were first asked both the first and second round of questions were more likely to agree to the second request than the fourth group of women. This indicates that the foot in the door approach is an effective persuasive technique.

The door in the face is the reverse of the previous option. This method states that after a hefty demand gets rejected, a smaller request is asked instead. The idea is that the unreasonable request will make the small request easier to accept. An example of this would be if an individual is working with a contractor who asks for a sizable amount of cash up front, but it is

decline. The contractor then comes back with a smaller number that is accepted.

A study was conducted in Austria where a saleswoman offered cheese to people who are walking by. The saleswoman first asked people for 4 euros for 1 pound of cheese. She then asked a second group for twice as many euros for 2 pounds of cheese. When the people said no, the saleswoman asked the second group for 4 euros for one pound of cheese. The study showed that the second group was twice as more likely to accept the cheese for 4 euros than the first group. The results showed that even though the majority of the first group thought that 4 euros were too high, the second group had a different point of view because of the initial higher price. Anchoring is the third persuasive technique. Pricing a common form of this. Companies will use this as a way to suggest a higher price than what a product typically sells for. Consumers will attempt to negotiate the price down to a point where they are getting a bargain price when in actuality; the product might normally sell for even lower than the bargained price. The idea behind this tactic centers around the decision-making process. For example, a woman is buying a necklace for $150 but manages to bargain the cost down to $100. When the woman gets home she sees that the necklace typically costs $80.

A real-world example of anchoring comes from a study done on MIT students. A well-known magazine had three different package options for customers, option A's cost provided only the online version and option B was more than double the cost of option A and only provided the printed version of the magazine. Option C cost the same as option B but provided both the online and print versions of the magazine. The number of people who chose option A was about one-fifth of the number of people who chose option C. The experiment took students from MIT and only provided them with either option A or option C, option B was completely removed as a possibility. The results showed that the number of people who chose option A was more than double the number of people who chose option C. The experiment showed that option B was used as the anchor to enhance the appeal of option C. The fourth option is commitment and consistency which occurs when someone is able to get another person to commit to a small action; as a result, the person being persuaded is more likely to commit to more later on. An example of this is brand loyalty. When a person finds a brand those appeals to their needs, they are more likely to stick with said brand and try out the new products that a company comes out with. Makeup brands and sports brands are a great instance of having repeat customers.

A real-life example of this took place with a makeup company. The brand was able to get loyal customers to post about their positive experience with the makeup for a chance to win a yearlong supply of the product. With the promotion, the company was able to market its products to possible new consumers.

The next persuasive technique is social proof which states that people tend to follow along with what other people are doing. Groupthink is a major component of this particular method. An example would be if employees at an ice cream shop add a dollar to their tip jar so that when customers order their ice cream, they are more likely to provide a tip when it appears other customers have already done so.

A social experiment was conducted to prove the effects of social proof. There was a line of people who were all asked to answer one question; however, only the last of the people in the line were not in on the experiment. Everyone before the final people gave the same but obviously wrong answer. Once it got down to the people not in on the study, they too began giving the wrong answer because it was easier to go along with the group.

Authority based persuasion suggests that

people are more trusting of powerful and wealthy people. Companies can use influential individuals to get new customers to start using their product. For example, if a small company makes it onto the cover of a well-known magazine, this will benefit their business. When people see that the well-known magazine is promoting a small company, their already loyal customers will automatically be trusting of the small business.

A famous example of this technique is the Stanly Milgram experiment where the person of authority was able to influence the teacher" to administer the shocks, even when the shocks appeared to be inflicting pain on the "learner". The study proved that the majority of people are likely to follow along with what an authority figure says must or should be done.

Scarcity occurs because people tend to desire what is only available for a short amount of time or if there is only a small number of a product left. This technique is widely used by numerous companies to drive their consumer's "want" factor. An example of this technique would be that when a new movie comes to theaters, Dairy Queen comes out with blizzard flavors that are only available for a short period of time. Customers have in mind that they have a shorter window to get their hands on the movie inspired blizzard, and as a result, they get the blizzard flavor while they can.

An experiment used students from a university to detect whether or not scarcity has an effect on products. The students were put into two groups. One group was told that a product was running out and the second group was told that there was still a large amount left of the product. The study was able to prove that the students were more likely to buy the product when it appeared only a small number was left of the merchandise.

Reciprocation focuses on the fact that society has taught people that when you are given something, you are expected to give something back in return. This technique can be useful because if someone feels inclined to return a favor, then it is more likely that the person will get what they want. For example, when going to CVS, if you are a member, you are given coupons after making the purchase. CVS is providing a form of reward for those customers who become members of their franchise.

A social experiment took place at a restaurant where one waiter provided pieces of chocolate to each of his customers. As a result, the waiter was given a decent tip. A second waiter also gave pieces of chocolate to each of his customers; however, this waiter came back with a second piece of chocolate for his customers. This waiter averaged a higher tipping rate than the first waiter.

POWER OF SUGGESTIONS

In this chapter, we will talk about ways we can send a strong suggestion, and after that, there will be some more interesting possibilities brought to us by the use of covert hypnosis. Introducing you to these concepts will help in recognizing the variety of situations in which you can apply the techniques learned.

Verbal suggestions

The most common way to send a suggestion is

through verbal means. However, people usually send verbal suggestions in a very direct, that is, obvious way. Say something or request something directly will certainly convey our message to the interviewee, but that does not mean that our suggestion in this way will be strong or convincing enough to be accepted by the other party. Let's see the following two examples:

• "Honey, you will be delighted to see what I cooked for lunch."
• "You will be tremendously excited when you realize all the possibilities of this digital camera. "

I will surely surprise you if I told you that both sentences were uttered so that they convey the suggestion in exactly the same way. However, though the content or context of the sentences is different, their structure is exactly the same: both sentences create or establish, the same feeling - expectation.

What makes it suggestive? Well think about it and you will understand that we usually get exactly what we expect. Very often we create ourselves "mini prophecies" and convince ourselves that we will like something, and something else we will not. And mostly when someone thinks he won't like something - he really doesn't like it. Vice versa. Beware, it doesn't even have to mean that he REALLY doesn't like it, but a man often so strongly suggests to himself that little prophecy, that when in reality he faces a completely different feeling, he simply dismisses it. Let's say, we offer someone to try spaghetti with seafood. He sees there are clams in it and refuses to try, claims that he doesn't like clams, they are disgusting to him, though he had never even tried them. You somehow manage to persuade him to try and he does. It tastes interesting, smells nice, but he nonetheless refuses and claims he does not like it. His reason and whispers: "Well, this is not bad at all," but the prejudice is so strong that he gives up. But it is almost certain that the next time he has an opportunity, he will accept the offered dish, just because of that previous pleasant experience he had.

So, when we "assume" something, we generally experience it. When you utter sentences like the ones at the beginning of the chapter, you are actually moving the thought processes of the interviewee in the direction of expecting what you suggested to him: that he would like what have you cooked or will be delighted with the capabilities of the digital camera. Because of this, there is a good chance that this person will just react the way you suggested to him. Not that it will literally "delight" or be "excited". These are just words that associate feelings with which you support your suggestion. What you want to achieve and what you will almost certainly achieve with these examples is that the person will LIKE what you offered him - so lunch or camera; of course, with the proviso that he is interested in it at all.

There will be plenty of examples of verbal suggestions in this book, but I note that the words you use are not the most important in communication. Very often, they are not even primary in order to successfully convey a suggestion.

Presentation is also very important, or the way you convey these words. If you convey the suggestion with enthusiasm and honesty, its strength will be far greater and vice versa: if what you are saying don't correspond with the signals your body is giving, it is unlikely that anyone will believe what you are claiming.

Non-verbal suggestions

Non-verbal suggestions are suggestions that we do not convey with words. Our gestures and facial expressions are what leave a strong impression on the interviewee. So does the "solidity" of speech and the way we emphasize something have a significant role in conveying a suggestion, especially when our interlocutor cannot see us (for example, when talking over the phone).

When you think about non-verbal methods, just remember what is the most common reason why some movies simply draw you into a story and another completely turn you down. This is of course acting. If the acting is not convincing and if the actors are bad, there is no story that will keep us with the movie, and not only that: when the story "pulls you in", when you are fooled by their acting, the movie will take you so much that you will lose your sense of time, maybe your legs will go numb, or you will even lose the feeling of a complete body. This is because you entered into a hypnotic state of deeply focused attention and high suggestibility, that is, in a mean hypnotic trance.

You have in your life many other examples similar to this one. Remember how many times, when talking to someone, you were sure that he was not telling the truth, just because he was unconvincing? On the other hand, you have certainly had situations where someone tells you something unbelievable, but with so much energy, he enjoys the story so much that it's hard not to believe it. Notice the next time someone talks convincingly and interestingly, how listeners will very quickly get into a hypnotic trance, which we just described, how will they relax the muscles in their face, calm their breathing and their eyes will shine. Non-verbal methods are used not only by experienced actors but also by successful marketers and skillful seducers and speakers (either because of Love or other benefits).

One of the most powerful non-verbal suggestion techniques is the so-called mirroring (that is, reflection), which represents copying of the interlocutor (that is, his posture and body movement). Given that people they like others similar to them when someone acts the same way, he actually sends a message: "we are alike", which helps the interviewee to relax, to be comfortable in his presence and therefore reduce any (conscious) resistance. By imitating the body of the interviewee, you are subconsciously telling him that you have something in common, which then leads to the development of trust.

Mirroring is part of a discipline we call rapport or subconscious connection and we will explain it separately. But if you want to play, here it is some tips:

• Never overdo it in the imitation of another person, because it can very easily become obvious and your interlocutor will realize that you are imitating him. Not only will this break your rapport, but it can also cause the other person's negative feelings and reactions.

• It is often sufficient to copy only one or two positions for the entire flow of conversations. The point is to send a signal that you are similar, and not to constantly giving attention to it.

• Always take a short break. When the interviewee, say, cleans up the throat and you want to copy it, do it after thirty seconds, that is, when it is your turn to speak.

• Rotate the position. If, for example, he puts his left hand on his side and his face is facing you, you also do it with your left hand. If you did it with the right, it would really be a position like in a mirror, while this way it is less noticeable and equally effective. This is otherwise referred to in the NLP as "matchmaking," or alignment.

Why is rapport important? Whatever the situation, the other person considers at the beginning, that is, that you are different. Your interviewee will subconsciously think, "we are different," because "he wants to sell me something," "because he wants to drag me in bed," "Because he wants to convince me of his version" and so on. Just by building a rapport and sending a subconscious message, "no, we're not different, we are exactly the same, " you change those thoughts into," he has a product that I need, "or in" this is a person who would be worth spending time with. "

Why is that so? Again a little psychology. We mostly can't resist ourselves, that is, our own actions and ideas. Therefore, when we meet someone who is the same as us, resisting that person is very difficult for us because we subconsciously experience it like we are resisting ourselves.

Another terrifying yet very understated way to absolutely, quickly and effectively overthrow any resistance is a SMILE. A smile sends a strong subconscious message that sounds like "I want to be your friend" or: "I don't mind getting closer." Smiling is especially effective in situations when we are in a company of a person who has an aversion or a negative opinion of us. With a smile, like something the first thing we show, and what that person will notice, we can not only "disarm" him, but even confuse him, which is also one very desirable hypnotic condition. Because when consciousness is confused, it then seeks for a solution, for something to guide it, for an answer to a question "what should I do now". And then when consciousness is too busy searching, the subconscious must take command at least for a moment and if at that moment we say something, then our words make it right into the subconscious, without any conscious analysis and criticism.

Let's say you are in a situation of approaching a group of friends, including the girl you like and you're sure that she isn't happy about you "coming to bother". Offering a hand, wide and honest smile and one "hello" will send a completely different, friendly picture of you. At the very least, that person will leave with one completely different impression of you and will be guaranteed to think about you for some time, trying to understand why is that you no longer seem so repulsive to her. In addition, if you recognize at the time of greeting that the person is confused but not "confused" in terms of whether or not to accept your hand for saying hello, but confused because this is a completely unexpected situation for her and she doesn't know how to act, you can then say something that it won't be invading, but it will be suggestive enough. For example, you can utter (with a smile, as a joke, but not with irony) the following sentence: "Greetings from the most beloved person in the world." Believe me, this is lascivious hypnosis at work. I must mention that unless you are sure that the person is really confused, be careful with suggestions. Not because they may have a different effect, but because you can make the person respond with something and you won't know for a moment what to say, and this will again cause you to get confused and lose the smile from your face, thus undoing everything you have achieved by then. So if you aren't sure, just smile, look her in the eye, say hello to her and then turn to the next person to say hello and continue the conversation.

Intraverbal suggestions

Intraverbal suggestions are something I mentioned at the beginning of the story about non-verbal suggestions. They are intonation, the way we emphasize and pronounce something. For if we pronounce the word in such a way that our statement reflects what the word itself means, so is the power of suggestion bigger.

For example, we can say that something is big, short, clear and precise. But if we say with ascending intonation that something is very large, we're making a completely different impression, aren't we? The very word "no" can be stated so that it means not only NO, but YES, and even MAYBE only depending on intonation. "Just imagine how happy you will be when you first influence someone subconsciously. "By emphasizing the word "Overjoyed", we initiate positive feelings (in this example, positive expectations as well) at the one we are addressing.

You have seen in simple examples how we can combine different techniques to send a suggestion. Now, I don't want you to be scared and think, 'who is going to master all this', because it is you who will master all these techniques, very easy and very fast. You will rarely be in a conversation in which you'll have to apply the whole arsenal of "hypnotic words and expressions". Mostly two, three phrases or two, three techniques are enough for the entire conversation. Like as noted above, you should send the message, not to constantly try reminding people of it. Of course, some suggestions will from time to time need further development or repeating, but I emphasize that it doesn't matter how often you do something, it only matters if it is noticeable or not. And your goal is the latter. In any case, let me say it again: the way in which something is said is often far more important than the spoken word itself. No matter how hypnotic it is.

Extraverbal suggestions

This way of sending a suggestion is extremely powerful. Of course, if it's properly implemented. The closest description of this kind of suggestion would be: "read between the lines ", or in our case:" speak between the lines ". These suggestions are most often a combination of the previous three groups and therefore they have the strongest effect, and the goal we want to achieve is that the listener accepts the suggested action as his own. Yes, to think it was his idea or desire. And when he thinks that, then that is something he can't oppose.

Take for example the situation where you have a business presentation in front of a few people and you are bothered by the noise coming through the open window. The easiest way would be to address someone and ask him to close the window, is it not? That person will almost certainly do it, however deep within he will feel that this was an execution of the command you had given him, it is again something that few like to do. We don't like anyone to command us, even if it sounds like a plea, right? However, if we use our knowledge of extraverbal suggestions and say something like, "I just hope you hear me, given the noise that comes from outside "this will cause someone to stand up and close the window. And not only that that person did what you wanted and subconsciously will not feel embarrassed because she had performed your command, but she will also figure that she did you a favor! And the favors are done to the people we care about, the favors are made by the people who love us, who we like, who are close to us, who are our friends - in other words, it is another step towards strong rapport.

Suggestions like this work because there is no reason why we would think we should resist them. Nobody told us anything, suggested, required, or asked us, these were all our ideas, ours the desire and the decision to do, or at least that's the way these suggestions affect us. Extraverbal suggestions actually initiate the thought in the listener's head, and that is his thought then - the only thing he doesn't know is that that's exactly the thing we wanted to do. And then, when the thought was born, he did also wished to turn it into action. And the goal has been achieved.

Play around with this for a little while, practice with your friends or in any situation that you think is appropriate. And another thing: whenever you have the opportunity to record some of the conversations you have with your client or acquaintance, do it, so you can analyze it later. Soon we'll talk about the best method for practicing these techniques and those recordings will be very useful. Do not forget that a "fair relationship" means you must have the consent of the other person if you intend to record your conversation.

COVERT HYPNOSIS

In this chapter, we will deal with some more ways in which we can send a strong suggestion, but above all the interesting possibilities that bring the use of (covert) hypnosis. Knowledge of these concepts will help you recognize the variety of situations in which you can apply the techniques learned.

Hypnotic trust

Although we have already made an introduction to subconscious links, or rapport, it is necessary to deal with this topic a little more. We all know what trust means, but what hypnotic trust really is, or what we think it is under this term? Remember the situation when you meet someone for the first time and you almost instantly like him. Although you have no reason for that, although you seemingly have no excuse, from the first encounter the person is extremely appealing to you. Or it's not. This phenomenon is called hypnotic trust.

Hypnotic trust (also mistrust) arises because a person does, or says something that reminds us of another person whom we have known for many years, we trust or like. Simply this new person subconsciously reminded us of someone and that is why we trust him without the possibility of consciously explaining why.

Contrary to this, remember if you have ever been in a situation that you or someone close to you is expecting a baby, so parents are trying to agree about the name. Then, for example, he says, "What if we name her Alice?", To which she answers: "Oh, no, I had one Alice in the class and she was very annoying!" What does this have to do with the child? None, of course. But subconscious memories are powerful enough to make us judge.

Leading marketers and other people who are successful in "convincing and persuading" surely apply this technique. Often they don't even know how it works, they just know it works. Trust is primary, in fact crucial element for any kind and form of hypnosis. Trust drives the mind into a state of high suggestiveness because it eliminates resistance; we have a tendency to listen and follow the people we trust and are less inclined to critically analyze their words and actions.

Take a look at the following example now. Let's say I ask you to write down what you think of me. In fact, why not, let's take a break, take a piece of paper and a pen and write in a few sentences what you think of me, and then continue with reading ...

... Most of you readers, who do not know me at all, will make your comment based of the text read so far, and your past experiences related to this topic, as well as personal wishes and expectations of what you will gain by reading this book. You have chosen
to read it and you hope it can help you achieve some of your goals and that is why you certainly want to believe that I am an expert, wise, intelligent and competent person. The point is that you probably know absolutely nothing about me, but you DECIDED to trust me and that's why you evaluated and commented me based on your prior experiences or current expectations (about what you'll gain from this book).

The point is that hypnotic confidence can be

built with just about anyone person, very easily and in very little time. It's enough that you are honest, that a person feels that he or she can rely on you: that you are trustworthy and you are a person of confidence. However, there are many situations in which trust must be built up quickly, and in these situations, the hypnotic techniques we will learn will be of much help. But for now, let's see first what other effects can we achieve by using covert hypnosis.

Ideasensory trans

This is also something we experience every day, and it represents the ability to imagine in our minds images, sounds, sense of touch, smells and tastes. Whenever we imagine "live pictures", whenever in our minds we recount or have a dialogue with someone, we are experiencing this effect. I remind you once again that we are not "in a trance" at the time, but we use the word "trans" as a substitute for the word "state." That means that in those moments you find yourself in a special state of mind. Often some people will say they don't believe that this is true of them, that they don't create pictures, that is, they don't imagine stuff. But this is not about imagination, we're not talking about that, it's about those occasional internal dialogues that almost each of us has.

Let's say you want to cook something for dinner and have no idea what to make. You look what groceries you have in the house and then you start thinking about how could they be used. You think of a dish and you don't want to make it, you are not in the mood for that today. Then something else comes to mind and you think, "Um, well, I haven't eaten that in a while, and I just love it." You just lived through an ideasensory trans. You have developed in your mind some idea of a condition, that is, information that you receive from one or any of your physical senses.

Or, say, that situation where you need to meet with someone and talk about something. You get nervous, not sure what to do and then in your head, you first begin to imagine the encounter, then the dialogue, thinking about what you would say and how would the other person respond, in the end, you even "see" their face and "hear" their voice. I think you get what I'm talking about.

Extremely suggestive people can evoke live images and other senses (sensual, like smell or sound ...) in their interlocutors. Let's say, a car salesman can suggest to a potential buyer to imagine himself on an empty highway, "squeezing the throttle all the way to feel the speed and power of an engine, "to imagine neighbors, turning their heads, pretending not to see his new car, "or his wife" accidentally calling her girlfriends for coffee" just for the sake of bragging and so on. And the potential buyer will imagine and experience all that without even buying a car. If you can evoke very realistic images and feelings in the interviewee, it will often be enough to achieve the desired goal, that is, to convey an idea or suggestion.

How to practice this, and what to say, what to suggest? It's very easy. Just put yourself in the position of the person you want to influence and try to understand what are the positives that they will get if they accept your offer. What benefits will they have, what will they feel or hear, what will they taste. And then suggest just that. But it is important to understand that it's not enough to just "list the positive things," you have to force your interlocutor to really "feel and experience" the situation they will find themselves in after they accept what you offered or try to sell them.

You can also suggest the negative consequences that they will have if they decide to "refuse you", that is, not to buy what you offer. A typical example is an antivirus program for computers. But you won't just tell the potential customer, "If a virus gets into your computer, it will wipe everything you stored in it," but you have to envoke in him images and emotions, for example: "Imagine it comes to data loss and a race to recover the system begins. And imagine a headache as you search for the most important data in the archives while you are constantly interrupted by phone calls from colleagues who are powerless and don't know what to do." You get the concept. Remember, we often only buy something just because of the negative ideasensory images, that is, just to avoid the negative consequences we assumed could happen. Assumed and then imagined in your mind.

Amnesia

Amnesia, in the context we are dealing with, does not signify memory loss, but another common hypnotic phenomenon, again present in everyday life. The simplest examples would be those situations when we can't remember our phone number or person's name we met recently. Or, for example, the name of a movie, and it's "on tip of our tongue". And we can use this phenomenon to subconsciously influence our interlocutor so that he would for a moment forget some information, our competition, the other offer, and similar things. Here's an example:

"It's almost impossible to manage yourself in a sea of unnecessary information and concepts that you'll find in other books on the subject of conversation and that is why we have decided to make them precise and systematic. "

With this sentence, I actually want to influence you to forget about competing books without directly mentioning them, I have an excellent "justification" for that because I suggested the "fact" that they just "flood you with the sea with unnecessary information." So, I'm not directly speaking negatively about competing products, as it would just cause a boomerang effect, that is, a negative attitude towards this book. In one of the following chapters, you will learn why.

Causing hypnotic amnesia in this way has one small limitation: it usually has an effect on individuals who are not detail-oriented. However, those interested in the details will want to hear specific facts. That's why with such people we should first find out what they are most interested in, and then use that information to "explain" to them how they can expect even more from us.

You may also find yourself talking to someone who already is under partial amnesia. For example, he was at a competitor or he watched a product similar to yours but can't quite remember the specific details. This situation will not mean that the job has already been done for you, rather, it is a fantastic opportunity to further deepen the amnesia, an example with words: "Well, it's quite normal that you don't remember, because who would remember all those details that they throw at you ... "and so on. And then, convincingly suggest the benefits of your product, for example by using ideasensory messages.

We stimulate amnesia with words and expressions such as: "forget", "difficult to remember", "impossible to remember", "irrelevant", "why waste time" et cetera. So if you remember the intraverbal communication and say those words with proper pronunciation, stretching them a little, suggesting in that way the "boredom" and "meaninglessness" of interest in such (competitive) products, there is your winning combination.

Hypermnesia

The opposite of amnesia, which controls what someone will forget, hypermnesia can make us remember some important information, fact, or trait. It is most effective when used in combination with ideasensory hypnosis, for example: "I understand you need to think about it more, to use our agency for your traveling arrangement, but I bet that when you go to bed tonight, put your head on a pillow and close your eyes, you will see yourself happily sunbathing on the beautiful beach while your feet are splashed with warm waves and you will wake up in the morning determined to spend the summer at sea. So, see you tomorrow. " In this way, we used one routine, such as going to bed

in such a cunning way that this person will almost certainly, when he lay in bed, really imagine himself on a vacation. And there he is in the morning, with a delighted expression, hurrying to tell us that we were right and, of course, at the same time book a vacation arrangement.

Words and expressions such as "you won't be able to forget", "unforgettable", "you won't be able to get it out of your mind", " you'll think about this all day", " you will remember this for the rest of your life" " you will forever remember "and so on, increase the likelihood that your interlocutor will connect pleasant associations with what you offer him, and consequently accept your offer.

"I'm sure you will remember this night all week and that every morning you'll be waking up smiling and thinking about when will Saturday come and will I make you laugh like this again. "

You can also "pass on" hypermnesia to another person: "Your wife will remember this day for the rest of her life when you made her so happy with this present." Or the story of an earlier, satisfied person can be used, for example, "who bought this product of ours a few years ago and who still remembers that moment today. "

You can also use it as a "negative" as an example telling the story of a person who, a few years back, had it such a bad experience on vacation that she has never forgotten the inconveniences that happened to her at the time and she decided that from now on she would only travel with trusted agencies like ours. " As you can note, there is no mention of a specific "competing travel agency" thus avoiding the development of unpleasant emotions but leaving strong, "negative" impression because of a problem that person experienced, what awakens the desire in the interviewee to "avoid such a situation" by choosing "a trusted agency like ours." You practically alerted the person to possible problems due to poor choices and then suggested the way they can avoid it. Totally honest, open and friendly.

Hypnotic dislocation

This is the ability to detach ourselves from the current environment. E.g, Remember the situation at a meeting, presentation, or school when you at one point completely stop listening and hear the one who is talking, thinking of something far away from the subject or the situation you are in. And then all of a sudden you were woken up by the question posted directly to you, and you have no idea what is the topic and what was discussed, so you need to ask them to repeat the question. Although you were physically present, you were not actually there but, in your mind, in a completely different place. You were in a state of hypnotic dislocations.

This phenomenon can be of great benefit when properly applied and it can divert the interlocutor's attention from the current environment, let's say that they don't pay attention to other people around them, what are they saying, car noise, phone rings and things alike. Dislocation is triggered by starting the sentence honestly by describing the situation, then suggesting to overcome it and ultimately what we want our interviewee to focus on. E.g:

"I see that your ex-boyfriend has come, which makes you nervous right now, but as that nervousness leaves you and disappears, you will be able to continue to enjoy yourself in this beautiful evening and we will have more fun than ever. "

Time distortion

Time distortion is another technique based on everyday experience. Each of us will say that "time passes quickly" when we are having fun, how is "staying still" when we are bored and there is nothing to do. Or remember how long two minutes lasts in the elevator and two minutes of watching an interesting movie, or an exciting match. Do they last the same? The same time unit can sometimes be infinitely long and sometimes never shorter.

You can use hypnotic techniques to influence how will your interlocutor feel, or experience time, that is, a period of time. If you need more time and there is a risk of making your presentation too long and boring for your interlocutor, you will make it seems short and fast. On the other hand, if you don't have enough time available, you can "slow it down" and have enough to convey your message.

"The next hour will be the fastest and most exciting sixty minutes you have experienced lately. I guarantee you will be delighted to see what opportunities you have and that time will fly".

Or for example:
"Relax, we have quite enough time to go slowly and peacefully through all the essential facts in the next ten minutes".

As you can see, we start the time distortion by suggestion with full self-confidence, about how our interlocutor will experience forthcoming time. When you do it with enough security and a desire to "get going and do", you also develop the appropriate expectation in your listener. And we already said that people generally get what they expect.

You can also use this that for you, your product, or your service you relate the feeling of "flying" time. Ask them to describe to you their favorite movie or book. By describing, that person will return to the past and relive the emotional state he or she was at the time, associated with the feeling that "time is flying." At the very end of describing make a slight transition to yourself or to what you offer. In that way, the positive emotions that this person has awakened will be related to you. And then, it will seem to people "like time flies by" in your company.

MANIPULATION TECHNIQUES

Similar to the persuasion techniques, the manipulation techniques are used to influence how another person reason and behave. When these techniques are utilized correctly, a person will not have even inkling that they are being manipulated. Some of the techniques are more effective once they are partnered with another technique and others can stand alone. However, with every one of the proceeding techniques, it is important to not get caught.

Fear and relief focus on the manipulation of another person's emotions, which is likely to cause an immense amount of stress and anxiety, but it is also extremely effective. The method comes in two parts, hence the title of the technique. The first part centers around the idea of fear. The individual using the technique will cause another person to fear something, which in turn brings out said person's vulnerabilities. The manipulator will then provide relief from the distress. The trickiest component of this technique is finding the best fear tactic. It is important to inflict fear based on a person's specific stressors. There must be an awareness of what to say and do in order to bring out an individual's vulnerabilities, but one must also be prepared with a way to replace the fear with relief. If the technique is done correctly, the switch between fear and relief causes a person to experience mood swings. As a result, the individual will become totally exposed. An instance of how this tactic can be used in the real-world can be found in the news at home. For example, when a station begins talking about an outbreak of the flu where some cases have resulted in death, people tend to become panicked. The news comes in with statements such as "stay tuned to hear how you can protect yourself." The news is providing the viewers with possible ways to keep themselves, as well as the people they care about, safe. A few other possible options are to use a personal relationship to get into a familiar mind, or bosses can use the technique to motive employees. The technique can be used completely selfish reasons, or to influence a positive outcome as well.

The second tactic is the mirroring technique and is one of the most well-known options. Similar to the previous technique, this too comes in two parts. At first, the person being manipulated is mirrored by the manipulator. The goal is to create a level of trust with the target that will hopefully allow for an in to exploit them. During the first part of this technique, the manipulator will focus on and match the other person's body language, the inflections of their voice, and their automatic reactions. It is important to remain subtle while doing so or the person being mirrored may become wary of the behavior because if not, the trust will be lost.

The second part of this technique involves the switch in who is being mirrored. The person being manipulated begins copying the manipulator. Once this happens, it is a sign that a complete level of trust has been established. It takes a great deal of patience to reach this portion of the tactic, but once the trust is there, some of the other manipulation techniques can take over.

Studies have been conducted to prove the effectiveness of the mirroring technique. One study was done during a business negotiation. The results indicated that better deals were made when the negotiator copied their coworkers. A different study was done in a restaurant setting where waitresses received higher percentages in tips after mirroring their customers. It is important to note that when mirroring is only used for a personal gain, the act can only last for so long before the person being manipulated begins seeing through the façade.

The next technique uses guilt, which is a tool used to psychologically manipulate an individual. When a person is experiencing guilt, they will likely try to compensate whichever way they can. The manipulator will come in and suggest their own idea for how to extinguish the guilt. The tactic is the most successful with people the manipulator has already developed a bond with, especially those who have already let the manipulator down in the past. The manipulator will go about influencing their target by slowly and patiently planting ideas into their unconscious mind until the person being manipulated believes those desires to be their own.

While this tactic appears to be one of the simpler and easier ones, a manipulator can run into trouble if it becomes obvious what is happening. It is important to be careful and choose the words and actions strategically to ensure that the target will not suspect the manipulation. When the technique is done correctly, an individual will do what they can to not see them self as an immoral person.

Although it seems as though guilt is strictly a negative use of manipulation, there are cases of positive guilt. For example, with the downfall of the ecosystem today, companies and organization are promoting the use of eco-friendly products. The promotions are not shy about putting the blame where it belongs, the human race. While human beings are the cause of the attack on the environment, they are also the solution. The use of guilt, in this case, is used to try to influence people to do better and save the environment.

The fourth technique focuses on playing the victim which is linked to the guilt approach. When a manipulator is acting like a victim, they are in turn forcing the target to feel ashamed. The manipulator would likely use phrases such as, "Why are you treating me this way?" or "Do you treat everyone this way, or is it just me?" Once the manipulator makes accusations of mistreatment, no matter how insignificant the resistance maybe, the person being manipulated will look back at their actions or words and be influenced into believing they have been ill-mannered. As a result, it will be easier for the manipulator to influence the individual to do what they want.

When using this approach, it is important to keep in mind that there are drawbacks at times if the manipulator overuses the victim card. One example of effective use of this technique is in an abusive relationship. The abuser will turn their aggressive actions around onto their victim. Say a woman was out with her friends and had forgotten to tell her partner, the abuser might strike his partner, they may suggest something like, and "You made me do it. If you had just said where you were, I wouldn't have been so worried." The abuse victim would believe they had done something wrong and would attempt to make it up to their partner. In this case, guilt plays a huge factor in the outcome of the manipulation.

This suggests that separately, the guilt and the victim techniques can work, but when to put together, they become their most effective.

The manipulation technique love bombing is commonly used by people with a narcissistic personality. The tactic plays heavily on the emotions of an individual by showering them with affection and being attentive to their wants and needs. This takes place at the beginning of a relationship with the person being influenced. The goal is to make it difficult for the manipulated individual to not see the good in the manipulator, even though the influencer's actions are a front. The victim is tricked into an emotional trap with the manipulator that leads to an intense and overwhelming feeling of affection for the manipulator.

This technique is most effective on particular individuals, specifically those who have a deep desire for love and attention. People who are lonely are also suitable target. It is important to keep the true intentions a secret or the bond will not be able to form between the manipulator and their victim. An example of this would be a cult. The members are overly kind and enthusiastic towards possible new members. The cult members are careful about hiding their intentions until after the proposed supporters have officially signed up as real members. After this point, it is too late to turn back because the influence has already taken over.

The sixth technique involves bribery. When a manipulator rewards an individual, that individual will feel obligated to return the favor in some way. The influencer takes advantage of their target's mental state to achieve their own desires. The tactic begins with discovering the desires of their victim so that the manipulator can meet said desires. The next step is to propose a favor in return. However, if the manipulator asks for the favor in a way that sounds threatening, the manipulation ends there. It is essential to keep the conversation light and have it appear the manipulator is simply being kind.

Bribery is believed to be the easiest manipulation technique if it is done properly. The most important component of this tactic is timing. The manipulator should give an individual what they want cautiously and only after a substantial amount of time has passed, should the manipulator collect their own request. By waiting, the manipulator is establishing trust with the person they are manipulation.

When bribery is put into practice, studies have shown that many of the manipulators provide small gestures of kindness and in return, they receive a more generous reward. Bribery can also take place over a longer period of time, like providing someone with discounted items. The person being manipulated will see their manipulator as someone who has been kind multiple times in the past, suggesting they should repay the favor. An example of the successful use of bribery is if an employee is looking for a promotion. Around Christmas time, the employee gives his boss an expensive watch and a few months later when the position opens up, he applies. The boss may remember the act of kindness from his employee and give him the position.

The next manipulation technique is ironically also a key component to any healthy relationship, being a good listener. However, the motives in manipulation are different than those for an honest relationship. For a manipulator, listening to another person is an essential component to be able to influence a said person. The art of being a listener has two main benefits for manipulators.

When a manipulator appears to be interested in learning about their target, it shows a level of friendliness that translates to being trustworthy. This is especially appealing to individuals who do not have social interactions often. No matter how long the conversations may go on for or how dry the exchange is, it is important to stay alert. The information divulged at the beginning is essential for the second portion of listening. There is a possible way to grow the trust between the manipulator and the person being manipulated so that influence can take place. If a manipulator recalls details that their target had spoken to them about, the target believes the manipulator listened to them because they truly cared about what the person being manipulated had to say.

An example would be if a real estate agent listens to a client while showing them possible rental locations. When the client comes back in for a second showing, the real estate agent may bring up the family vacation the client said his family was going on. The act of listening and appearing to care, maybe what closes the deal for the real estate agent.

Another manipulation technique is to psychologically and emotionally exam reading body language. What a person says with their body can be more reliable than a person's actual words. It is easier to conceal the truth with words than it is with the human body because body language tends to be an involuntary reaction that a person is unaware they are doing.

Reading body language is not a difficult task; however, it is imperative to recognize the meaning behind different types of body language. When a person has their arms crossed over their chest, this usually indicates they are feeling defensive or disengaging from the conversation. If an individual has their head tilted to the side, this may indicate they are listening intently to the conversation. When a person has their fingertips pressed together but their palms are apart, this signifies the person is showing signs of authority and power over others. People who stand with their back straight imply a high level of confidence. Eye contact is a tool used to create a comfortable environment. For example, in an interrogation room, a detective will read the body language of a possible suspect to pick up on any sign of guilt or unease. If the suspect signals a guilty conscience, the detective will push for more information in the hopes of nailing down a conviction.While manipulators can use body language to read a situation and the emotions of a particular person, they can also use some of their own body languages to influence other people. Manipulators can use eye contact to ensure a level of trust from another person. A manipulator can also use standing up straight or having their fingertips together to put them self in a place of power over someone else.

The next manipulation technique of playing with another person's feelings is an easy way to influence a said person. The idea behind this tactic is that once a person develops a strong emotional connection, especially a loving one, it becomes easier to force them into thinking emotionally rather than rationally. As a result, a manipulator is able to influence a person into doing whatever they want.

The trick to achieving a type of connection is to first master one's own emotions. If a person attempting to manipulate is not in tune with their own emotions, they may run the risk of being the one who gets manipulated. Fear and sympathy are both strong sentiments that come into play during an emotional connection, and both the person being manipulated and the manipulator them self can fall victim to these emotions. A real-world example of this approach would be through marketing. Companies try to appeal to their loyal customers about the new products a company has produced. Apple comes out with new high-tech phones that their most loyal customers are waiting in line to pick up. Even though a person's current phone works perfectly fine, their desire for the new merchandise outweighs the logical side of the brain.

The final manipulation technique is all about using a person's looks to their advantage. No matter how hard people try to deny it, good-looking and charismatic individuals are easier to trust. However, good-looks can only get a manipulator so far. It is crucial to marry the beauty with the actual strategy. The previous technique is helpful tools to couple with good-looks. Positive use of body language can promote comfort. Making a person feels special and giving a slight air of confidence is also beneficial for an attractive manipulator.

A well-known, but a sinister example is Ted Bundy. The serial killer was notorious for his good looks and his ability to lure a woman away before murdering them. He was a college-educated man with a charming smile. The man was able to take a woman in broad daylight in public places without setting off any alarm bells from people. Even after he was caught, it was difficult for police, prison guards, and citizens to believe such an attractive man could have been behind the brutal killings. Bundy was even able to marry after being arrested for at least 30 murders. The man manipulated every person he came into contact with, but in the end, the law still won.

MANIPULATION IN RELATIONSHIP

The use of manipulation in a relationship is one of the most effective uses of the con. As previously stated, when there is an emotional connection between two people, it becomes easier to influence their thoughts and behaviors. If a person is concerned they are being manipulated, there are telltale signs to be aware of. Some of the signs are identical to the manipulation techniques discussed in the previous chapter, yet others are unique to a close relationship between people.

The main problem with being controlled in a relationship is that the manipulator is able to slyly shift any argument in favor of the manipulator. Once every mistake or fight is put onto one person, that individual will lose sight of their own thoughts or actions. The manipulator will then have complete control over the entire relationship, to the point where the person being manipulated cannot see a way out of the relationship.

Abusive and controlling partners are infamous for using certain tactics to influence their partners. If a person can note any of the following signs, it is important to get out of the relationship safely before the manipulation escalates.

Playing the victim is also one of the manipulation techniques stated in the previous chapter. When an abuser or controlling partner is utilizing this technique, they are never in the wrong. It always seems to be the victim who is apologizing. The goal for the manipulator is to force their victim to feel unworthy or guilt-ridden over instances while the influencer avoids any backlash for their own actions.

When there is an argument between a manipulator and their partner, the manipulator will ignore any of their own faults and place all of the blame on their partner. The schemer begins making statements such as, "why are you hurting me?" or "you're breaking my heart, are you trying to upset me?" This forces the victim to take care of the manipulator and completely abandon their own emotions.

If an individual finds them self in a situation like this there are ways to protect one's self from their manipulator. One option is to only apologize for what they truly believe they could have done wrong. Do not give in to the manipulator's words of belittlement. Stand strong and say something along the lines of "I am sorry for what I said, but you hurt me too. This is how you've made me feel." This ensures both partners are held accountable for their separate faults.

The next sign is regular bullying. This particular sign can be easier to spot; however, it does not make it easier to walk away from. The fear of what a manipulator might do is what compels their partner to do as they are told. The manipulator will make it appear that they are simply asking for assistance, but a look or gesture will say otherwise. For example, a controlling partner might say something like, "could you go get me a beer?" Their words alone are not what coerce the victim to obey; it is the dark and menacing look in their eyes that dares their partner to challenge them. After the manipulated partner gets the beer, the manipulator will respond as though they did not need to get the beer. As a result, the victim begins to believe their actions were completely voluntary.

When a person finds them self being bullied by their partner, sometimes it can be safer to do what is asked. Once the act is completed, that is when the victim can begin looking for a way out of a similar future situation. It depends upon who the manipulator is. If the partner is abusive, they will likely use violence to get their victim to comply. However, if the manipulator is not violent, it is wise to begin asserting one's self by saying "no" to requests. It is important to note that if a person cannot feel secure with saying no and standing their ground against their partner, they need to leave the relationship.

Taking a partner to a place that is out of their comfort zone is another sign of a controlling relationship. Manipulative partners are likely to choose where they and their companion go and who they interact with. The goal here is to control the level of comfort their partner is able to feel and to, more importantly, keep them self-

feel secure.

If a person is questioning whether or not they are being manipulated in their relationship, look at where the pair goes on dates, who's friends they interact with and who's home they spend time at. This signals that the victim is tangled up in the controlling partner's life, but the manipulator has no interest in their partner's life. Once a person sees this type of relationship, stand up for what is equal. Do not settle for anything less than what is fair. It is key to making sure both partners are deciding where to go on dates and interact with both partner's friend groups. This will ensure that everyone's level of comfort is evenly balanced. Another sign is when a partner plays with the emotions of their significant other. In a healthy relationship, partners discuss and talk through situations. For example, if a chef walks by a building that has been put up for rent, it would be reasonable for him and his partner to discuss whether they can afford to rent out space. If it had been a manipulative partner who came upon that building, there would be no discussion. The controlling partner would make it seem as though their significant other is an immoral and cruel person if they had reservations about renting the property.

If a person is in this type of situation do not

give in to the pressure. It is important to do what is best for one's self and not their manipulator. Provide an alternative option that can prove your kindness. For example, in the case of the restaurant, suggest that the partner go in with a partner so that the money is divided between two people. By turning the tables and putting the choice onto the manipulator, the victim appears to be on their partner's side.

The next sign of proving one's love is extremely conniving. The idea is that the victim is compelled to prove their love for their controlling partner repeatedly. The manipulator will make a statement such as, "If you really loved me, you would stay here with me tonight and not go out." Or even, "If you want to prove you love me, then make me some dinner." When phrase such as these are used, the manipulator is using guilt and emotional brainwashing to get their partner to do what they want.

The best way to stand up to this sign of relationship manipulation is to turn it down. This can be done by countering the manipulator's statements with, "I do love you, but I already made a promise to my friends" or "I love you so much, let's make dinner together." It is also an option to call the partner out on what they are doing. Saying something like, "You don't have to profess your love to get me to cook you know."

A statement such as that lets the manipulator know that their partner is aware of the manipulation and as a result, the tactic will no longer be used.

The next sign of manipulation in a relationship is all about emotional coercion. During this sign, a controlling partner will ultimately use fear and guilt to blackmail their significant other to stay with them. A manipulative partner may threaten to harm them self if their loved one were to leave them. By uttering a statement such as, "If you leave, I'll kill myself." Or they might say something like, "I can't live without you." The manipulator's goal is to place responsibility on their partner so that they will be fearful of what could happen if they were to walk away from the controlling partner.

When a person finds them self in a situation similar to this one, it is important to remember that they are not responsible for their partner's life. While a manipulator's threat to harm them self is more often than not only a ploy, it is also wise to make a small threat of one's own. The person who is being controlled can reply to their partner's threat with, "If you are going to hurt yourself, I am going to call 911, but I cannot stay here and be with you." The words may seem insensitive, but is likely the only way to get out of the situation without anyone being injured.

Gaslighting is an extremely dangerous sign of manipulation that can make a person feel as though they are going crazy. A controlling partner will do something shifty on a daily basis. These types of partners will deny having said something that they did, in fact, say, the partner is likely to pretend the partner being manipulated did not make certain comments as well. If a partner leaves out information, stretches the truth in their favor, and cause a partner to question their own mind, they are definitely displaying signs of manipulative behavior. If the lies and deception occur over a lengthy amount of time, the partner being manipulated will lose faith and trust in their own mind, and as a result, depending on the controlling partner for the "truth".

If someone or someone they know is experiencing gaslighting, get out. Do not try to work through the problem. Gaslighting is a powerful and conniving tool that can be extremely harmful to a person's mental state. Seeking professional help to work through the mental effects can also be helpful once an individual has safely gotten out of the relationship.

A surprising sign of manipulation is opportunistic neediness. When a manipulative partner is not getting what they want, they might begin to feel ill. One example would be if a controlling partner does not want their significant other to go out with their friends. The manipulator would say they are experiencing high levels of anxiety, but after the victim agrees to stay home, their manipulator remarkably recovers. A controlling partner also uses this tactic to get extra attention from their domestic partner. The sole purpose of either scenario is for the controlling partner to get what they want.

If an individual finds them self in a needy relationship, consider leaving. These types of relationships are not healthy ones. Leaving the relationship at the very moment a partner is conveniently in need of assistance may not be the best time. However, one can arrange for their partner's care while the manipulated partner gets done what they need to. The manipulator is likely to be just fine while their partner is gone.

When a partner is being "killed with kindness", it may be a sign of manipulation. A controlling partner has ulterior motives behind being kind to their partner, which can be difficult to detect at times. Manipulators use their words and charm to hide their true motives. For example, if a partner says, "You are so talented; I don't know why you don't take the job." While on the surface, the partner appears to be motivating their significant other, they are actually planting an idea that fits their own desires. A manipulator will not take into consideration whether their partner would be happy at the other job, as long as it pays more.

One way a person can protect them self from this sign of manipulation is to thank them of their kindness, but not give in to what their controlling partner wants. It is imperative to note that manipulative kindness is not an actual act of kindness, it simply a means to get what the manipulator wants.

Another sign of manipulation is if a partner is constantly calm, cool and collected. When a situation would typically cause some type of reaction but a partner remains completely calm, manipulation is quite possibly taking place. The idea behind this sign is for the person being manipulated appears to be overreacting. This can cause a person to feel as though they cannot trust their own emotions and reasoning which can later lead to the manipulator having competed for control over their partner's emotions. The manipulator controls whether a situation permits an emotional reaction. If the victim goes against their manipulator, they will be made to feel their reaction was unnecessary or dramatic. Manipulators will even begin questioning their significant other's mental state and reliability. Once a person's mind is called into question enough times, they will begin to look to their controller for how to respond.

If a person finds them self in a relationship with mind games such as these, therapy can be extremely helpful. When a person cannot trust their own mind, it is imperative they seek help to reconnect with their own emotional responses. It is important to remember that no one has to justify their emotional responses to anyone else.

The last sign of relationship manipulation is when a significant other is always "joking". This jokes that a manipulator uses are no laughing matter, they're the only goal is to belittle and weaken their victim. The use of "jokes" comes in two parts. Part one focuses on criticizing their significant other but questioning why the partner becomes upset. The manipulator will say they were only joking, and the person being manipulated is too sensitive.

During the second part, the manipulative partner will "joke" when there is an audience. The controlling partner will make jokes about their significant other in a way that judges their appearance or actions. For example, a controlling partner might say "Honey I almost forgot you were here, you're so small." If the victim responds to a comment like that in a negative way, they are making a scene and embarrassing them self. This allows the manipulative partner to take jabs at their partner without having to suffer any consequences.

However, if a person finds them self in a relationship with a lot of "joking" from one partner, do not be afraid to stand up for one's self. Even if it will "ruin the fun", no one deserves to feel belittled and ashamed. Be aware that standing up to a manipulator is likely to result in a few more digs, but know that what they say is not the truth. Talk to friends and family about what one is dealing with to help build confidence back up. If an individual is experiencing any one of the above signs of manipulation in a relationship, it is time to speak up and regain self-worth. It is also a wise decision to get out of the relationship altogether because manipulative relationships are not healthy and can be extremely damaging.

A romantic relationship is not the only instance where an emotional connection leads to manipulation, family members have also learned to influence their loved ones. Manipulation that takes place within a household can be more hazardous than when it is done by a domestic partner. The previous examples stated about manipulation in romantic relationships and how to safely leave those relationships are moot when a mother, father, or sibling is the manipulator. It is often not feasible to think that completely cutting out a family member from one's life. When the whole family gets together, it is likely that the victim and the manipulative family member will be in the same room. However, there is a way to make a family reunion more enjoyable even in the presence of an influencer.

Before looking into ways to prevent further manipulation from a family member, one must first understand whether or not manipulation is actually taking place. One sign of family manipulation is excessive lies. When someone is able to lie easily, this can be an indicator that they are a controlling person. These types of family members may also respond to direct questions with vague answers.

A chronic liar is also known to provide people with half-truths in an attempt to trick people into thinking that they are honest and reliable people. A deceiver will also try to cover up their past lies with new ones. Their deceptions are a ploy to achieve their own desires at the expense of the people around them.

The use of the silent treatment is another way manipulative family members gain control. In fact, the closer two family members are, the more likely this tactic will be used. The goal of the approach is to force another person to meet the manipulator's needs without saying a single word.

The victim of the manipulation will often beg and plead with their influencer in order to end the silence. In the end, the manipulator has their desires met and the victim is consumed with guilt.

The next sign of family manipulation is fake selflessness. The manipulator's goal is to appear to be a reliable and noble individual who can be trusted. The controlling individual is motivated by knowing that the people around them will think highly of them even though their "selfless" actions are only a cover for the greedy desires. The manipulator sits back and watches everyone praise them and soaks in the fact that they have gotten exactly what they wanted, their family member's trust.

Gaslighting is common in romantic relationships, but it can also be harmful in a family dynamic.

Intimidation can be one of the most difficult signs to pinpoint among siblings. It is common for, say a brother, is pick on their younger sister to show her who is in charge. However, there is a fine line between sibling rivalries and actual traumatizing. Manipulation in the form of intimidation is almost never an actual threat, but rather using fear to force a family member to do what they want. The intimidation tends to be blanketed by a false sense of kindness that makes it seem as though a family member is looking out for the best interest of their victim. In actuality, the manipulator is only concerned with their own needs being met. By paying close attention to the words a family member uses, their true intentions may be revealed unintentionally.

A manipulator's use of guilt-tripping is used regularly by coercive family members. If a controlling family member is told the word "no", they will look for any opportunity to make their target feel remorseful for not going along with their manipulative family member. An example of this tactic is if a father asks his child to turn the TV volume down, the child will turn the TV off altogether in order to ensure a sense of guilt. This particular tactic is used to make a person empathize with the manipulator, which allows the controlling, individual to gain control over a situation.

Shaming is one of the most disturbing uses of manipulation in a family. Normally, family members aim to protect and lift their loved ones; however, the controlling, and often narcissistic type of family member will do the opposite. Their goal is to exploit their loved one's weaknesses and insecurities to gain superiority. For example, if a sister is insecure about her weight, her sibling will take every chance she gets to poke fun of her sister's weight. This constant berating, allows the manipulator to maintain control over their family member.

Once a person has gathered all of the necessary facts and has come to the conclusion that they are being manipulated by a family member, it is time to prevent any further manipulation. One way to do so is to look around at other family members and see if they too are being manipulated by the same person. When all of the victims have been pinpointed, the next step is to create a dialogue among all of the people being affected by the controlling individual. The discussion can center around what boundaries the manipulator has been overstepping and what types of behavior is negatively impacting the other people in the family.

The family should then implement a solution to help stop the loved one from continuing to manipulate. It may be difficult for the manipulator to understand why they cannot control and influence the people around them, and more importantly, why it is wrong for them to manipulate. It is vital that the manipulator is taught that controlling other people to the point where they are no longer making their own decisions is not healthy for either party. If the manipulator is unable to wrap their head around no longer manipulating their family, there are steps that can be taken to keep the manipulator at a safe distance as well.

A victim of family manipulation should take a moment and look into their own mind because manipulator's bend the truth to meet their own needs. If the victim of a manipulator is able to search through the lies and find the truth within their own mind, they are taking back some of the control the manipulator is seeking. An individual's ability to dissect their own emotions, thoughts, and actions is key to weeding out the foreign concepts implanted by a manipulator. Before a victim of manipulation speaks they should also stop to make sure their opinions have been created by their own free will and not through the influence of someone else.

Setting boundaries with a manipulative family member is one of the most effective ways to protect one's self from further mind manipulation. Controlling individuals tend to act like the victim in order to get the person they are manipulating to act without thinking to resolve the situation. If a person identifies this cycle with a loved one, this is not the time to set the boundaries. The reason being, when someone finds them self in a defensive position, it is easier for them to fall prey to manipulator's trap.

Instead of acting at the moment, a person

should take a step back and look at the entire situation. During this time, the victim should remain calm and polite towards the manipulator but articulate clearly the boundaries that need to be installed within the relationship. There is no exact right moment when an individual should take the step to set boundaries, but choosing a time when the victim can keep their emotions in check is an extremely beneficial point to pick.

Understanding the best place to set boundaries is also important to take notice of. Manipulative family members tend to choose large family gathering and reunions to play the victim so that there are many witnesses to their target appearing to be the "bad guy" in a given situation. It is vital that the person being manipulated does not fall into the trap and act out in any way. Instead, they can create their boundaries without uttering a single word. The target of the family manipulator can refuse to engage in the defensive behavior that the manipulator intended to bring out. When a manipulator's victim remains calm and level headed, it becomes difficult for them to be manipulated.

One final way a person can coexist with a family manipulator is by being the bigger person. It can be difficult to set aside the frustration and hurt once a person learns that a loved one has been manipulating them, but it is important to not let them have any more control over the victim's mind. It is also imperative that the victim thinks of the other people in the family because manipulators typically are unable to take responsibility for their faults. It is up to the victim sadly to keep the family from falling apart.

By not feeding into a manipulative family member's traps, the rest of the family will begin to see the truth as well. The real culprit of family drama will come into focus and the other family members will take notice of the negative emotions the manipulator has instilled in them as well. Once the rest of the family has seen the truth, they will follow the initial victim's lead and set boundaries with the manipulator. If enough of the family does so, the controlling loved one will be forced to behave in a socially acceptable manner.

While it can be difficult to learn a loved one is has been manipulating their family, it is important to remember that the rest of the family can stick together to change the negative behavior and create a more healthy household dynamic.

There are certain warning signs to look out for that can lead to manipulation separate from the signs found in a romantic or domestic relationship. If an individual finds them they are in the presence of a manipulator, there are also options for how to prevent any further manipulation.

The first sign is a manipulator will want to hear about the life of the person being manipulated. The goal of this ploy is to discover the strengths or weaknesses of the other person so that a manipulator can exploit them. An example of this would be if, on a first date, the manipulator asks questions about the other person. The manipulator will provide a small and most likely insignificant piece of information about them self before steering the conversation back onto the individual being manipulated. A statement like "enough about me tell me more about you" can be a red flag if it used too often. One important point to note is that manipulators tend to repeat the action of listening extensively to other people. If the person being manipulated becomes aware of the ulterior motive, they can begin choosing not to divulge any more about them self.

A manipulator may also attempt to confuse people by providing an overload of facts on a topic. The goal here is to establish a level of credibility that in turn enables them to control a given situation. Car dealers are a great example of this method of action. When looking at a car, the dealer will describe all of the features it has and overloads a person's brain with facts until it seems as though the person has to buy the car, or they will be missing out on a great offer. Car dealers exude a level of confidence that can trick people into spending more money than initially planned on. When a person finds them self in a situation similar to this one, it is best to leave the conversation and gather one's own information to maintain personal control.

Another sign is a manipulator's tone of voice. Some manipulators will raise their voice in an aggressive manner to force someone to conform to the manipulator's desires. An example of this form of manipulation is an abuser may aggressively suggest that their partner is only going out with their friends in order to cheat. The victim will feel forced to prove this is not true by staying in and canceling on their friends. If this situation occurs, it is best to remain calm and walk away or say "no" to the demands being made. The next sign plays on the weaknesses of a person. The manipulator will attempt to generate insincerities in another person through the use of humor and sarcasm. Common ways manipulators do this is by jabbing at a person's appearance, personality, or habits. A manipulator may say something like "Honey I don't think you need that second cookie, do you?" Or "wow you must be on your period; you are way too sensitive right now." Either calmly tell the person that speaking to people in such a negative way is uncalled for, or simply walk away and do not let their unkind words sink in if one finds them self in a situation like this.

Since manipulators are unable to take responsibility for their actions, they will often remain ignorant about any consequences to their actions. The passive-aggressive tool is used to avoid obligations that do not match the manipulator's wants and needs. A manipulator may say something like, "It isn't my fault. You made me do it." Or "You're just being too sensitive" when they find themselves in an argument, specifically one where they are in the wrong. This type of manipulation is also extremely common in the workplace. If an individual sees this type of manipulation, stay confident and refuse to give in to their lies. Carefully attempt to ensure the manipulator is being held accountable for their faults.

In relation to avoiding obligations, manipulators may also place blame onto other people. This is a common occurrence when manipulators stretch the truth or "forget" essential facts. The manipulator's compulsion to tell a fib is seen as one of their greatest weaknesses. An example of this would be if a manipulator was caught lying about where they were, they may suggest that they *did* tell their partner where they were going and the manipulator was just misunderstood. Do not give in to the lies and walk away. People who have an inability, to tell the truth, are often described as pathological and can be extremely harmful to the mental states of the people around them. One final sign is if an individual creates a false sense of urgency for another person to make a decision. As a result, the person being manipulated will have their decision-making process negatively affected, which leaders to the manipulator being in complete control of the situation. For example, fast food companies such as Dairy Queen, McDonald's, and Kentucky Fried Chicken created products that are only limited time; however, the time frame is usually not indicated. This causes people to believe that if they do not go out right away, they will miss out on the product. However, there are also cases where manipulators will use this tactic that only benefits them. If a person notices signs of false urgency, get out of the situation and refuse to be a part of this type of mental game.

LYING TIPS

Unless you're a compulsive liar or a professional con artist (honestly, we hope you're neither), you probably find that lying doesn't come naturally to you. Let's be clear: that's a good thing.

Now, we'd never encourage you to take up the dark art of deceit, but there are cases in which lying is actually a good thing, and it would behoove you to be a little better at it. To help you out, we asked people whose jobs it is to assess whether someone is being honest with them— CIA officers, poker champs, law enforcement officials, therapists, and more—to get their insights on how to avoid getting caught when you're trying to tell a whopper. So read on, and good luck!

1.Trust Your Skills

One of the biggest ways to give away that you aren't telling the truth is when you lose your confidence and convince yourself that the person you are lying to knows you aren't giving them a straight answer. In fact, there's a good chance they have no idea, and if you just trust yourself you'll likely get away with it.

"Humans only correctly identify lies at a rate of about 50 percent," says Andrew Bustamante, a former covert CIA officer who lived undercover for nearly a decade. "That means there is always the 'shadow of doubt' when someone tries to assess whether you are lying or being truthful. Remember that you have the advantage because only you know with 100-percent certainty that you are lying."

2.Stick to Your Story

This might seem obvious, but even the smallest adjustment to your story is likely to raise suspicions in a skeptical listener. "If you change anything about your original story, you introduce contradiction and degrade credibility," says Bustamante. "Even bold-faced lying will be accepted as 'possible truth' as long as you keep your story consistent. Don't believe me? Watch the debates between Barack Obama and Mitt Romney in 2012."

Know what your story is down to the smallest details, and don't veer away from it from one telling to the next.

3.Keep Your Lies Believable

Bustamante emphasizes that in general "people always assume honesty"—but only if your lies are believable.

"Keep your lies within the realm of reality and you will nearly always convince the person sitting across from you," says Bustamante. "Lie about your age within five years, your height within two inches, and your salary within $15k and nobody will ever catch you."

4.Avoid Knowing Things You Don't Want to Reveal

One of the best ways to avoid looking like a liar is to not know whether you are lying at all.

"Professional poker players will deny information to themselves so that they can't reveal any secret information," says Michael Josem, a poker security expert.

He gives the example of a pro poker player

who might not even look at their cards until it is their turn to act, so that even if they had a bad habit of subtle reactions to their cards, players who have to act earlier can't learn anything from them.

"Similarly, they can avoid looking at community cards until it is their turn—and instead spend that time focused on observing opponents," he says.

5.Keep Your Mouth Shut

Another effective way to avoid being caught in a lie is to keep your chit-chat to a minimum. Only say what you absolutely must, reducing the chances that you'll say something suspicious—or that your body language will give you away.

"If you're playing poker against a sophisticated opponent, in general, you will want to reduce the information that you give to them," says Josem. "Rather than try to trick someone or lie to them, you are much better off to minimize the amount of information you give, than to try to trick them."

6.Respect Repetition

Body language is often a deadlier giveaway than any words coming out of your mouth, so just as you want to minimize your conversation, the same is true of your body language. Act natural, but keep your movements limited.

"Fundamentally, poker is a game of information, and the more information you give to an opponent, the more likely they'll make a good decision," says Josem. "Thus, two sophisticated players will try to control their bodies to behave in a very repetitive manner each hand—so that as little information as possible is being given off."

7.Ground Statements in Truth

If you're going to lie, keep as much of it as true as you can.

"Within your story, the foundation and many of the facts should be something that is true and something you know well," says Laura MacLeod, a therapist and HR expert and creator of From the Inside Out Project.

She gives the example of your running late to meet with your partner, perhaps because you've been shopping and spending more money than they would like. The story you tell your partner can include your trip to the store, your purchase of necessary items and/or your attempt to find necessary items and maybe that the store was crowded and you had to wait in line—everything except the overspending you did at the cash register.

"The point is you can sell this," says MacLeod. "You know the store, what they sell, how crowded it can get, inefficiency of clerks, etc. When you speak about what you know, it's easier to commit to it. When you commit, your listener will too."

8.Keep it Light

Defensiveness is a dead giveaway that you have something to hide. If the person you are speaking with raises questions about your story, keep things light, cheery, and casual.

"If you are questioned, smile," says MacLeod. "This immediately takes the heat off you and paints you as totally innocent. Attempt to help the listener get it: 'Not sure what you don't understand. You know how slow those clerks are at X store—remember the time we waited 15 minutes to get a price?' Getting the attention off you and using what you know throws your listener off."

9.Breathe

Fidgeting, swallowing often, or showing a general sense of tension are some typical nonverbal ways that liars reveal themselves, according to Ashley B. Hampton, Ph.D., a licensed psychologist and owner of Psychology, Consulting, & Evaluations, LLC. And one of the most effective ways to get these tics under control? Steady breathing.

"Breathing slowly helps reduce anxiety, which will help with the sweaty palms and the feeling of cottonmouth making someone swallow often," she says.

10.Be Present

"Being in the moment and focusing on the conversation is one way to help reduce blood pressure and eyes darting around the room," adds Hampton.

If you can stay fully focused on the person you are speaking with and feel present, rather than distracted or preoccupied, the information you are conveying will come across as much more congruent and believable.

11.Stick to the Subject

According to body language expert Patti Wood, author of Snap: Making the Most of First

Impressions and Charisma, habitual liars are likely to switch the subject when they've been caught in a lie or when the person they speak with raises questions about their version of events.

"Truth tellers won't give up the conversation until they convince the person who thought they were lying that they're telling the truth," she says. "Liars want to change the subject and end the conversation, saying, 'I don't want to talk about it' or try to switch the subject or distract the person."

12.Avoid Categorical Statements

Similar to changing the subject, liars will tend toward oversimplifications or absolute statements, according to Wood, who gives examples like, "I would never lie," or, "I'm not that kind of person," as the kind of flimsy defense you might hear from someone who is not being entirely honest. Instead, a more nuanced response to the specific issue being questioned is more likely to be perceived as honest.

13.Answer Questions with Questions

A good liar only lies as a last resort. Instead of issuing an utter falsity, they'll answer a question with another question. Here's an example: Let's say you're asked point-blank about some less-than-commendable behavior—stuff you most certainly did, but might like to deny. ("Did you really blow a grand on those boots?")

Instead of outright saying something simple and deniable like, "No way!," retort with something along the lines of, "C'mon, how dumb do you think I am?" Chances are, your inquisitor will drop the topic on the spot. They wouldn't want to insult your intelligence, now, would they?

14.Make Sure It's Not Verifiably False

Don't offer up any facts that could easily be double checked, and proved wrong, says Bruce Hurwitz, a recruiter and career counselor, who gives the example of claiming you were late "because of an accident" when a few questions or a check of the traffic report could reveal that no accident happened along the route you claimed it did.

"That's the beauty of the 'My dog ate my homework' lie," he says. "Go prove it!"

15.Maintain Eye Contact

"You must be able to 'sell' the lie," says Hurwitz. "You must make and maintain eye contact and have good posture. If you look away, or your shoulders droop, or you fidget, that can be interpreted as a sign of nervousness or lack of confidence. Honest people do not need to be nervous and do not lack confidence."

16.Maintain Your Facial Expression

Likewise, you should not be making wide-ranging or fast-changing facial expressions if you want to be believed.

"Do not change your facial expression," says Hurwitz. "If you believe that the person to whom you are speaking believes your lie, and you smile, that may give the lie away."

17.Go With Your Gut

"If people overthink their lie—if they are overly conscious that they are lying—then it becomes too much pressure and they get flustered, and the deception becomes obvious," Neil Wood, a former undercover cop, told Vice News. "If you have to think about it too much, that's what gives you away."

In other words, there's no need to do a ton of homework on a mark. There's no need to memorize a hundred canned statements and contingency phrases. Just, in the moment, go with your gut. If you've internalized the preceding advice, the lies will flow like water—and no one will suspect a thing.

IMPLANTING THOUGHTS

Manipulation can be found in a multitude of subtle instances including seemingly innocent conversation and the sharing of thoughts and ideas. The lack of awareness that a master manipulator can strike during the simplest of encounters is one of the many reasons why controlling people are so dangerous. Knowing that a person can alter another person's thoughts and reasoning without notice can seem rather chilling, but it is done every day.

Manipulators use their refined skills to get what they want another person to believe by implanting their own thoughts into someone else's head. There are three ways a manipulator can get the job done, the first being reverse psychology. Since this form of psychology is widely used on TV, people tend to think they know all there is to know about the technique; however, it is also known that TV plays around with the truth.

When a successful manipulator attempts to reel a person into their reverse psychology trap, they are able to trick anyone into the more expensive deal. For example, say a salesman is selling flat-screen TVs. He will show a possible customer the top-shelf option first and tell a story about how a friend of theirs just bought this exact model. The TV was all anyone talked about at the house warming party just a couple of weeks ago. The real trick here is the salesman will speak about the TV as though he himself is longing to own one. Then, when the customer is about to take the bait, the salesman offers to show a cheaper model. The man will act as though it is no problem at all, but the customer cannot seem to fathom the idea of looking at a lessor model. The customer has already made up their mind on which TV to purchase, the one that will do the most damage to their wallet.

Another way a manipulator implants thoughts into other's minds is by talking their way around an idea. There are always reasons for why an individual should not go along with an idea and there is always at least one reason for why a person should go along with an idea. However, the best manipulators will not touch on either topic. Master manipulators talk in general terms about ideas to keep a person open to the possibility.

With the downsides, the manipulator will wait until the person being manipulated brings up the snags. From there, the manipulator will question whether a solution can be made. An example of this would be if a couple is looking for a new apartment. They may comment on the small size of the bedroom to the real estate agent, to which the agent could counter with, "Oh. You don't think that you can get everything to fit in there?" The couple would not want to seem as though they have too many items to fit so they might respond back with, "Actually, I'm sure we can make it work." The real-estate agent has created a situation where the couple is the ones behind the idea of fixing the problem and so, they are more likely to follow through than if the idea came from someone else.

The final way manipulators implant thoughts is through underselling. During this manipulative process, the person in control will truly make it seem as though they are promoting a decent cheap product or providing an option with minimal effort attached to it. However, what is actually happening is the manipulator is feeding a person thoughts of uncertainty to the point where the person being manipulated believes they need the more expensive or time-consuming option. Ultimately the manipulator is using underselling to get the outcome that matches their own want while making it seem as though the decision comes solely from the person being manipulated.

This form of manipulation can also be used by real estate agents. Say a young couple is looking to buy a house and they are on a tight budget. The properties being looked at are smaller homes that fit the price range. A real-estate agent would bring the couples to the desired properties but will make comments such as, "This house is very cozy, as long as the pair aren't looking to have any children." The agent might go on to say the couple can always look for a bigger house with rooms for kids later on. The newlywed couple probably has already discussed that they would like to have kids within the next couple of years. The couple begins wondering if they should look at a property that has more rooms for if family members come to visit and for when they have kids. It would end up costing more money to buy this house and then buy a larger home in just a couple of years.

The real-estate agent seemed to be looking out for the couple but ended up filling their heads with anxiety. Eventually, the agent had the couple thought it was necessary to look at a bigger house.

Aside from implanting manipulative thoughts into other people minds, another option is to control a person through "harmless" conversation. When a manipulative person engages in small talk, they are actually studying the person they are conversing with. As two people discuss something as basic as the weather, the manipulator is preparing to slyly learn who the other person is and more importantly, how to control them.The way a manipulator goes about this is by starting light and working their way towards those deep conversations. For example, two people are talking about the weather. Then, the manipulator steers the conversation toward what the weather can be like around the world. From there the manipulator is learning about the weather in different places the person being manipulated has visited. As well as who the target has met in the past, and maybe where they hope to visit later in life. With the help of some light conversation, this opens the door to get to know a stranger on a level that otherwise would not have been possible.

Countless studies have been conducted on the effectiveness of small talk and its ability to draw people together. One study was done on a train where a group of people was asked to engage in conversation with the people around them, and a second group was asked to avoid any type of exchange with people. The results found that even the introverts on the train preferred sitting by the chatty people over the quiet people.With the conclusions from the study, scientists and psychologists worked together find the major benefits of small talk. One advantage of small talk is its ability to calm a person who is nervous. If an individual is uncomfortable or unfamiliar with their surroundings, going through social conventions, such as informal conversation, allows a person to shift their focus to someone else. The mind alters from thoughts of *I don't know what to say* to *I can say "hi" and ask about their day*.

If a person has a difficult time engaging in small talk, think of it as a way to help someone else. By forcing one's self to come out of their shell, they are allowing someone else to open up as well. This bold move enables a person to become open to connecting with other people and in turn, develop relationships with the people around them. While the first two benefits to small talk can be useful in a typical exchange between people, a manipulative person will look for a personal gain. When a manipulative person sees a sign of weakness, they cannot help but exploit it. In this case, the manipulative individual will try to be that source of comfort for an anxious individual. As a result, a level of trust will be built that the manipulator can abuse.

When not in the presence of a manipulator, the second benefit to small talk is its ability to bring people together in the current moment. When two people are talking and they find common ground, the pair will begin feeling as though they are sharing an experience. The topic can be as simple as an interest in the same genre of music. The relation could also be significant, maybe they went to the same college. With either example, a connection is built between two acquaintances.

However, there are times when the common ground is a lie. A manipulator will ask a person about their likes and dislike, and the controlling person expresses the same interests. A manipulator may say something like, "You like

Radiohead? Me too! What's your favorite album?" The best manipulators know that people have an easier time connecting with those who share common interests with them. A manipulative person attempts to trick another individual into believing they actually have the same opinions by bringing up facts about the topic.

There are signs people can look out for that enable a person to weed out the liars. The first being the specific language the manipulator uses. If a person is a little off with the terminology regarding a particular topic, they may not know as much about the subject as they are letting on. The other red flag is if a person provides facts that do not quite match the truth if the only information being brought up is basic common knowledge.If either of these red flags comes into question, an individual can ask specific questions about the topic. When the manipulative person cannot provide the proper response, they will try to casually divert the conversation to a new topic.

However, if a manipulator is able to sneak their way into someone's life and develop an emotional bond with said person, picking up on manipulative comments and phrases can become increasingly more difficult. There are common phrases that manipulators use to appear as though they are harmless, but in actuality, they are taking control of a person's mind.

The phrase, "Look what you made me do" is used to make a manipulator appear as though they do not have control of their actions. The goal is to make it seem like the victim is the one who is controlling what the manipulator does, which creates a level of sympathy for the manipulator. The victim becomes hyperaware of their own words and actions and will often justify that the blame should be put on them.

One example of the use of the phrase is during the aftermath of abuse. The abuser will try to justify their violent outburst by stating that the victim is to blame for the behavior. If the victim had not done or said something wrong, then the abuser would not have struck them. This scenario is sadly one of the leading reasons why abuse victims have a difficult time leaving a violent partner. They are manipulated into believing that the abuse will stop if they manage to not offend or anger their partner. Yet, this is not the truth. Abusers will always find an excuse to take control and release their anger out on their partner no matter how small the reason.

If a person finds them self at the brunt of the above phrase, there are two great ways to keep the blame where it belongs, on the manipulator. The first options are geared towards a more violent manipulator. The victim should mentally tell them self that they are not to blame for their manipulator's actions. They should then take the first chance they get to seek professional help from law enforcement and a counselor. The second option is for manipulators who do not pose an imminent danger. The victim can counter the manipulative statement with something along the lines of "I am not the reason why you did that." By keeping the blame on the manipulator and standing one's ground, the controlling individual is forced to be held accountable for their actions.

The second phrase used by manipulators is stating that their victim is "acting crazy." The goal here is to get into the victim's head and have them believe that they do not know what they are saying or doing. The manipulator wants to appear to be "right" in any given situation so that they can eventually influence the responses of their victim in other situations. Manipulators may also use this phrase to avoid confrontation. When a person tries to bring up an issue they have with a manipulator, saying "you are crazy" forces the victim to let go of the argument and the manipulator is not held accountable for their actions.

The best way to respond to a manipulator in this instance is to remain calm and composed. Maybe take a couple of deep breaths, but be sure to speak clearly and rationally when trying to get one's point across to a manipulator. Do not get caught up in proving who is right and who is wrong, stay focused on the facts from the situation or conversation being discussed.

The third common phrased used by manipulators is saying "you are overthinking things." these words can be extremely effective because they suggest the person being manipulated is acting dramatic or imagining a problem that does not exist. Manipulators also use that phrase after they have deliberately upset the manipulated victim, which allows them to avoid any consequences for their behavior. It is also important to note that this phrase could be a gateway to gaslighting, one of the most psychologically damaging manipulation tactics.

If a person is told that they are overthinking, self-reflect and decide for one's self. It is critical that they trust their gut instinct and not back down from their manipulator. If the victim responds back by saying that they are in fact *not* overthinking and is actually thinking rationally, the manipulator is being forced to come to terms with their mistakes. It is important to attempt to hold a manipulator accountable for their actions whenever given the opportunity.

The final phrase used by manipulators is one

people long to hear from people who have hurt them, "I'm sorry." Manipulators love using this phrase because they can act poorly and fake an apology which creates a reason for why a victim will keep a manipulator in their life. Manipulators will apologize repeated but not change their behavior for the better. However, they still manage to make it appear as though they are trying to change, but in reality, they will stay the same.

If a person finds them self being reeled back in by the "I'm sorry" bluff, take a moment and think. What are the chances that the person will actually change this time? The answer probably isn't reassuring. Instead of giving a manipulator another chance, try thanking them for the apology but stating that it cannot be accepted until a positive change in their behavior is evident. A victim's ability to learn how to say "no" to a manipulator is one of the greatest weapons to have because it means the person is saying "no" to being controlled or influenced.

MIND GAMES

We play mind games because it makes us feel powerful and allows us to avoid taking responsibility for our feelings. The drawback of playing mind games is that you never really have an authentic relationship with people and thus never feel a deep loving connection that comes from honesty and trust.

Below are seven common mind games.

1 – Disqualifying. This is a method of saying something hurtful to someone and then, when they become hurt, doing a double-whammy by making it seem you didn't at all mean what they thought you meant. You may say to someone, "Sometimes you're so gullible." If the person becomes hurt (which you consciously or unconsciously want), you reply, "Oh, I was just

joking. Sometimes you're so over-sensitive." Not only do you hurt them once, but you hurt them twice, by disqualifying what you first said and then insulting them. This can make the other person both angry and confused.

2 – Forgetting. Passive-aggressive personalities play this game. Basically they forget important things like appointments, promises, paying back loans and the like. You wait for them to remember but they don't, and when you bring it up they reply, "Oh, I'm so sorry, I forgot." After having to bring it up several times you start to get annoyed. Then they reply, "Oh, I'm really sorry. Are you angry? You seem angry." If you ask them if they're angry at you, they protest, "Oh, God no. If I were I'd tell you." They make you feel that you're angry over nothing, which makes you more angry. This is how they "dump" their anger onto you without giving you a chance to voice your own anger.

3 – Persecuting. Sometimes people project their hatred onto others and persecute them. They are either unaware of their own hatred or they think it's justified. Once they begin projecting, they look for reasons to persecute. If the hated individuals disagree with them on politics, decline an invitation or smile the wrong way, the persecutor finds a way to punish them. They may talk trash about them behind their

backs, get others to gang up against them, or speak to them in a condescending or insulting way. They judge them as bad or evil and treat them accordingly. They never discuss their feelings or try to work things out. This is the opposite of the golden rule, "Do unto others as you would have them do unto you." This could be stated, "Punish others for not being what you want them to be."

4 – Guilt-Tripping. The game here is to make someone feel guilty unless they do what you want them to do. A wife calls her husband a "sexist," and at first he may protest, but eventually, in order not to be a sexist, he tries to be the kind of husband she wants. A husband tells his wife she's frigid because he wants her to feel guilty about not having sex with him. Thus, instead of simply saying to one's spouse, "It makes me feel hurt when you do such and such," which would lead to a discussion that might require both to look at themselves objectively, one simply calls the other a name and arouses guilt while avoiding reality.

5 – Gas-lighting. The term "gas-lighting" comes from the classic movie with Ingrid Bergman, in which her husband tries to make her think she's going crazy because she's seeing things (such as the gas lights going on and off). When she sees the lights going on and off, he says he doesn't see that at all. Some very

disturbed people use this technique on a hated relative. They say and do things and then deny they ever said them. When their partner persists in bringing up these things, the gas-lighter begins to question the other's sanity. "I think maybe you have an over-active imagination, my dear." At time the disturbed person isn't even conscious he or she is doing it.

6 – Shaming. People who play the shaming game express their anger by looking to catch people they don't like saying or doing something they consider inappropriate. It is the opposite of idealizing someone; it is demonizing someone. A militant religious person may wait for those who are not religious to say the "wrong thing." "Religion isn't always good," someone might say. The religious nut might then jump on them as they would a monster, distribute their quote all over the internet in an outraged tone and demand an apology. This game enables the shamer to dump his or her anger while looking to all the world like an innocent, concerned citizen.

7 – Pretending. Pretending can take various forms. A man can pretend to be interested in a woman in order to get laid. A woman can pretend to be attracted to a man in order to lead him on, thereby acting out anger. People can pretend they're not angry when in fact that are very angry. People can pretend to be your best friend in

order to get you to trust them while they hide their real motives. Good pretenders are good actors. Sometimes they even convince themselves that they're sincere. In psychoanalysis we call that a reaction-formation. A person may be jealous of you but deny it to himself and convince himself of the opposite, that he wishes the best for you. If you believe such a person, you may fall into their trap and regret it. Pretending is a way of controlling you and avoiding any confrontation that might result from honesty.

These mind games are bad enough when they occur among adults, but unfortunately some parents unwittingly play these games with their children, leaving them hurt and confused. These games all have advantages, but at the same time they prevent authentic relating and love, which are truly what make life worth living. Stay away from those who play these games and lean towards those who don't.

MIND CONTROL AND NLP

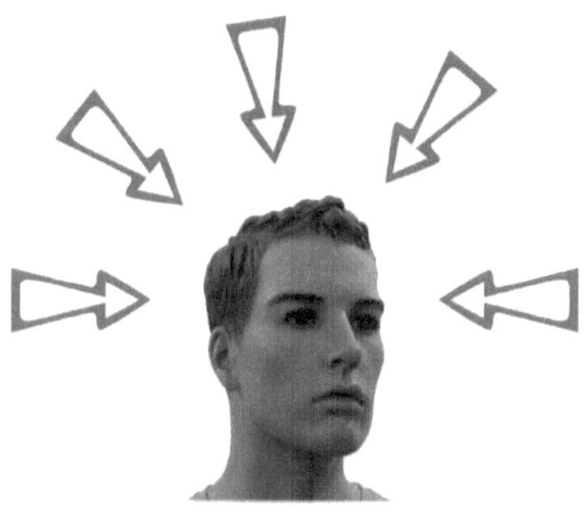

The question of whether or not complete mind control is possible is still being debated to this day. With the constant advances in technology, the topic seems to no longer be a possibility. A study that has not received enough attention is the brain-to-brain interface where one person's brain activity is recorded and is sent to a computer. From there, the signals are sent to another person's brain which ultimately matches the first person's brain. The year 2013 was the first successful recording of information being transferred from one brain to another.

While some brain-to-brain studies have found success, there are still limitations that need to be worked through. Complex thoughts and idea have not made the transfer between to brains because the complete understanding of consciousness is still being examined. The question of whether or not a brain-to-brain interface is ethical is also currently a topic of discussion. As a result, complete mind control has not been reached.

For now, mind control exists in the form of influence. There are psychological techniques studies both professionals about how to persuade other people to do what one wants. A field that benefits from this form of mind control is marketing. Marketing is all about motivating people to say "yes" in order to reach success. By the time a marketer hears the word "yes" enough times, their business is thriving. The opposite is true for those companies who fail to hear that magic word.

To reach success, there are certain strategies that can be utilized to control the consumer's minds. The first one is to think for the consumers because people already have too much on their minds. If a person is asked to think something over, but it does not end up being high on their priority list, they will not give it much thought or forget about the topic altogether.

To avoid this, rather than expecting a consumer to reason how a product will benefit them, explain and offer examples *for* them. Also, rather than asking someone to host their own promotion for the company's product, provide them with all of the necessary information and resources needed. This way, all of the material has been put in front of them and now they only have to talk about the product. Finally, do not beg a consumer to create their own endorsement of a product. Instead, provide the consumer with an example of other endorsements to guide them. Overall, the goal here is to avoid asking for help, but advise someone to assist instead.

The second strategy is to create a metaphorical avalanche. The idea is that successful marketers search and work through the most rewarding "yes" to then effectively break through the other "yeses" that will follow. For example, once an aspiring writer gets a positive response from well-known and respected writer, other authors and consumers will begin taking notice of one's written work.

It is a common misconception that marketers should start small and work their way up. However, in the long run, it creates unnecessary efforts. If a marketer starts from the top, the work that follows will be lighters and the end results are grander.

The well-known phrase, "give an inch, and they'll take a mile" is directly linked to the third strategy. When a skilled marketer asks for anything, they start small to ensure that it is easier to get started. Once it goes well, ask for more. Then some more, and don't stop until the marketer has gotten everything they need.

An example of this strategy can be seen in the classroom. Teachers ask their students to meet deadlines for portions of large papers rather than turning in the entire project without checking in. When a teacher or professor uses this approach, they are breaking down the project into sections until the work is completed.

The fourth strategy is to give the consumer more than what is taken. The common misconception is that the relationship between marketer and consumer is 50/50, but the smartest marketers give at least double what the consumer does. For example, if a marketer is looking for a YouTuber to promote their products, give them a generous number of products to try. The idea here is that the consumer won't be able to say "no" to the offer being provided to them.

The marketers who use mind control to influence consumers, the marketers who do not give up on the value of their products, are the one who hears that magic word "yes". While marketing is not the only form of mind control, it is one of the most effective uses of the technique.

In contrast to marketing, on the surface, Neuro-Linguistic Programming may appear to be a form of mind control, but in actuality, the thoughts and perceptions brought to light already live within an individual's mind. The idea behind this form of the programming focuses on the changes in perception and choices of responses through communication and situations. Whether the situation is in a personal or professional setting, each individual is given a choice that allows them to be responsible for their actions.

When a person goes through Neuro-Linguistic Programming, a therapist will have that individual dive deep into their unconscious mind where they will filter through layers of perceptions and attitudes. The goal is to discover what early childhood experiences played a significant role in what behavioral patterns a person has currently. NLP suggests that everyone has all of the resources needed to created positive changes in one's life.

It is significant that anyone considering the use of NLP knows that it is not necessary for a therapist to know any major details about a person's obstacle. This means that the particular event or issue does not need to be discussed with the counselor, so privacy is maintained. A non-discloser agreement is also signed by both parties, keeping any results and conversations confidential.

Neuro-Linguistic Programming is a noninvasive technique that allows individuals to find alternative ways to work through emotional hurdles including low self-esteem, coping with losses, and anxiety. The programming originated from behavioral science and specifically focuses on the unconscious mind and physiology.

Neuro-Linguistic Programming is becoming a more widely discussed topic because of how a deeper understanding of the unconscious mind can benefit people. The connection between the two minds is the conscious mindsets the goals and the unconscious mindset out to achieve said goals.

One example of the positive results found with using Neuro-Linguistic Programming is that it has help people beat their battle with addiction. A counselor can assist an addict by diving into their unconscious mind and discovering how that person views the world. It is common to see addiction as a way to cope with negative emotions a person in dealing with internally. Once the negative thoughts have been located, the goal then becomes trying to change the viewpoint to a positive one. As a result, the reasons behind the addictive behavior being altered to fight the need for a substance.

NLP is still being discussed and reviewed, but with some of its positive benefits thus far, the programming may be on the rise.

SKILLS OF A MANIPULATOR

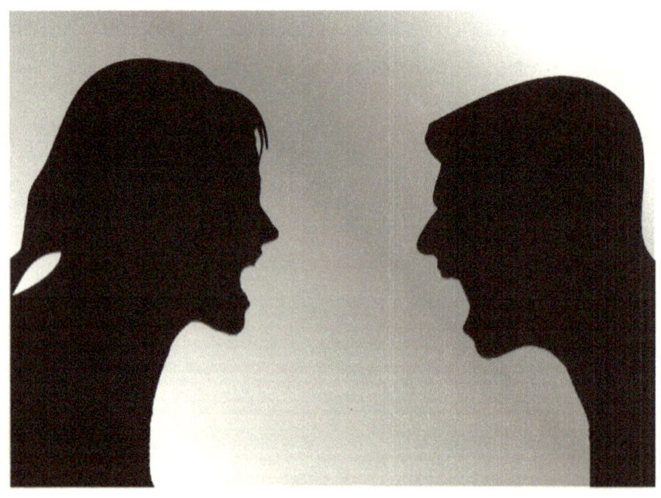

One of the most unnerving abilities of a manipulative person is their ability to control a person without giving away information about themselves. The most advanced manipulators have mastered the art of using the people around them before they are used themselves. An option for how manipulators prevent their own manipulation is they act above the people around them. By acting superior to another person, the manipulator is creating a dynamic that enforces their control over someone else. The manipulator can act as though they are more knowledgeable or more mature than someone else, and they can also use condescending remarks to weaken the other person's self-esteem.

Along with acting superior to someone else, they also can use physical intimidation to stake dominance over someone else. When a manipulator is oozing with confidence accompanied by their strong build or above average height, they can intimidate people into compliance. The majority of the time, the compliant individual feels too threatened to return the favor. The physical dominance over someone else is along the lines of bullying, which is another tactic manipulators use to take command of a situation. Manipulators can also prevent their own manipulation by being unreasonably difficult. When a manipulator knows that another person is seeking their approval, they will do whatever it takes to withhold that approval. The more a person tries to agree with a manipulator, the more the manipulator will disagree with that said person.

The manipulator basically agrees with the opposite of someone else. If someone says "up", the manipulator will say "down." The goal of the manipulator here is to argue with another person to the point of total submission. The manipulator is ensuring that their own thoughts and ideas stay completely separate from those of another person.

The final tool that is used is based on one-sided dependency. Manipulative people thrive on getting others to trust them. However, they refuse to give that same trust back to someone. This allows the manipulator to know the strengths and weaknesses of someone else without ever giving away any of their own assets and limitations. As a result, the person in control has all of the information on someone, while their own secrets remain in the dark. The best manipulators know how to take what they want from someone, without giving anything back in return.

Before a manipulator can reach expert status, they must first learn the basics for how to prepare for manipulation. The use of good verbal skills, a positive overall appearance, and the knowledge of psychology and neuroscience is what allows a manipulator to hone in on the techniques and strategies of the master manipulators.

When a person has the proper skills in

communication, they are able to skillfully articulate what they are influencing someone else to do or think. There are multiple ways a person can improve their verbal skills that will lead to the successful manipulation of someone. The first option may come as a surprise, but should not be overlooked. An individual is advised to become well-read to broaden their vocabulary. The books can cover topics of interest for whoever is attempting to manipulate; however, it is important to choose novels that challenge a person's mind. Choosing a simple book that can be found on the shelf of a middle school library is not going to benefit someone who is serious about influencing the people around them.

Reading more books is also a way for a person to become more versatile in the knowledge of different topics. One of the best tools a manipulator can have is knowledge because they can make other people feel inferior for not having the same level of understanding about a topic as the manipulator does. The manipulator is also not limited to novels; they can improve their skills from magazines, newspapers, and online current events. It is vital that an aspiring manipulator does not think of this form of preparation as boring, but look at it as an advantage they will have over other people.

Along with reading, a manipulator should

watch and become comfortable with how they talk. The best way to do so is to look into a mirror and begin speaking. While doing so, the person will begin noticing certain mannerisms, facial expressions, gestures they do not like. It is highly like the person they try to manipulate will not enjoy them either so it is best to change the negative details about them to one that people will respond positively to. A mirror is also a place where an ambitious manipulator can practice speaking to the people they intend to influence. This enables the manipulator to feel well-rehearsed before actually conversing with whoever they manipulate.

While practicing with the mirror, the manipulator should also begin working on the inflections and tone of their voice. They can record them self-speaking to pinpoint the positive and negative aspects of their voice. When a person speaks in an effective tone, it becomes significantly easier for them to mentally manipulate other people. It is pointless to try to manipulate using a timid, uncertain or monotonous tone. The key to an influential voice is to have it be confident and concise. The more practice that is put in, the more self-assured the manipulator will be when they speak to other individuals.

The next basic tool to master before

manipulating someone is making sure one is giving off a polished appearance. While genetics play a role in a person's presence, there are other ways for an aspiring manipulator to advance their looks. One possibility should be considered by every human, basic hygiene. People are more appealing when they give off a pleasant scent, it is an evolutionary fact. For centuries, the people who were seen as clean were the people it was safe to be around, and the mindset has not diminished with time. If someone plans on manipulating someone, stop by the local convenient store and pick up some soap. It's nearly impossible to influence someone's mind if all they can think about is how much the wannabe manipulator stinks.

Looking beyond smelling nice, if a person plans to manipulate someone, having a decent haircut is something to consider. It is critical to choose a hairstyle that specifically suits the manipulator because it will have a direct effect on the rest of their ensemble. At first glance, the idea may seem frivolous, but in actuality, it is right in line with a person's eyesight. When a manipulator is speaking, the person they are trying to influence will more often than not, take notice of the person's hair. It is important to reiterate that the hairstyle should match that particular manipulator. If the hairdo does not, then let it go and find one that does complement them.

Accompanying the hairstyle is the proper outfit that adds to the hairdo. This does not require the manipulator to be up-to-date on what styles are trending, a simple and classic look will work just fine. If the intended target does not appreciate the manipulator's look, then it becomes increasingly difficult to influence them. It may seem as though looks do not play too much of a factor in a person's ability to influence others, but in actuality, it is the first step to gaining their target's trust.

The final basic tool to learn when preparing to manipulate is developing a deeper understanding of the psychological and neuroscience processes. A fundamental understanding of the human mind before trying to manipulate one may seem like an obvious step, but it is also one that is easy to forget. Before learning the tips, tricks, and techniques to manipulation, the human mind must be examined. The way in which a person can go about learning more is by going on the computer and searching the internet. There are numerous articles with the sole focus of understanding the human mind. A variety of studies have also been conducted to prove theories and answer questions about the components that make up the brain. Checking out videos and reading psychology textbooks are some other great options to learn more about the mind.

When a person has worked through the groundwork to manipulation, it is time to put the plan into action and begin influencing their person of choice.

CONFIDENCE

There a plenty of cases where a manipulator is called out for their lies and controlling behavior, which results in the manipulator backing down and looking for a new victim. However, it is essential for people to remember that there are manipulators, such as physical abusers, who can become violent if their victim sheds light on their lies. If a person is in a situation where there is a concern that their manipulator might become physically aggressive, do not anger them. Simply go to the authorities, reach out to a counselor, and seek the support of family and friends. Let a professional handle the futile person and keep one's self out of harm's way.

Aside from the hostile and physically dangerous manipulators, there are common reactions that manipulators portray once they have been caught in the act of manipulating. For example, the most elusive and cunning manipulators do not break character. The most skilled manipulators can work through confrontation and make the victim appear to be the irrational person in the situation. Once the manipulation victim begins acting out and not thinking rationally, the manipulator will attempt to swoop in and regain control over the person.

When a person tries to defend them self against a manipulator, the outcome is typically not ideal.

When a person is in the moment, the thrill of having control and getting what a person wants can be enjoyable. However, chronic manipulation does not come without its drawbacks. It can be challenging for manipulators to develop healthy relationships of any kind. As a result, manipulators can lead a lonely life. In the workplace, an employee's reputation can be destroyed after lies and deceptions become known. This can result in missed opportunities in the workplace because other employees and the manipulator's superiors have a lack of trust for the controlling employee.

The manipulators who are able to experience some type of emotional response to their actions can begin experiencing a negative mental response including a guilty conscience. Aside from guilt, a manipulator may experience anxiety and stress because they are constantly having to cover-up and maintain their lies. The fear of getting caught in a lie can weigh heavily on the mind of a manipulator.

Along with the possible mistakes and hardships, a manipulator can find themselves in; the actual characteristics of a manipulator can play a part in whether they successfully influence the people around them. The master manipulators exude a level of confidence that can make the people around them feel inferior. However, typically, it is all a façade. Manipulators tend to have extremely low self-esteem, which if not hidden well, can prevent their ability to control a person or situation. Furthermore, manipulation can only go unnoticed for so long, and so sooner or later, people will pick up on the true intention of the manipulator and they will be forced to be alone. Being alone is actually one of the main fears of manipulative people.

Manipulators are constantly surrounded by people. They thrive on their interactions with people, specifically when they are the center of attention. Manipulators have an inability to have self-love because their desires come from the control they have over someone else.

There is an opportunity for an individual to match fake confidence with authentic confidence. One way to boost someone's confidence is to embrace what makes a person unique. Everyone has flaws, but they are a part of what makes each individual person stand out from the people around them. It is also key to not shy away from the quirks, but stand proud of who one is and everything that makes them who they are. Another tool one can use to build confidence is to not focus on the positives rather than the negatives. Everyone sets goals, but not every goal can be met right away. It is important to stay patient and positive about tomorrow while also be accepting of what has happened today. If a person becomes too focused on the setbacks and the mistakes, then that negative attitude can consume a person's mind to the point where they have lost assurance in their abilities.

Going for a walk is another way to boost a

person's confidence. While taking the time to clear the mind and relax, also take in your surroundings, specifically the people. Acknowledging strangers with a smile and a "hello" can calm a person down while also feeding the soul positive energy. Taking a chance on a stranger can be rewarding for both parties because more often than not the stranger will smile and say "hello" back.

When a person takes the time to say something nice to them self, it forces the person to recognize the positive attributes about that person. It can be nice to receive compliments from other people but it is even more mentally beneficial to hear them from oneself. Doing something nice for someone else can also positively affect both people's self-esteem. Take notice of the friend's in one's life and see who is in need of cheering up. One can help a friend by lending a hand on a project or complementing them. Acknowledge what their friendship means to the person can also do wonders for the friend's confidence level.

If a person is feeling down about them self it can seem impossible to see the positives, but it is key to try and be proud of one's skills. Take the time to think about what skills make one unique compared to other people. The attributes a person is able to acknowledge are the ones that make a person their own strong and independent individual.

One final way to boost a person's confidence is by making something, no matter how small or big, the benefits are instrumental. This ensures that the person is continuing to learn new things and challenging their mind. They could try making a new meal for dinner or build a birdhouse for their front porch. Either way, when the person has successfully completed a task, they are reminded of what they are capable of when they put their mind to something.

Once a person takes the steps to become a confident and contented individual, they are ready to take on the best of the manipulators.

10 Easy Ways to Boost Your Self-Esteem

1 Act as if you have confidence

While this idea may seem illogical if you have not yet acquired this trait, this is a shortcut to success.

If you act like you are confident, your attitude and body language will show that you really have confidence. Then, once you realize that it's not difficult at all, you're halfway to building this trait as part of your personality.

Keep your body upright, straighten your back, sit properly and look your interlocutor in the eye during the interaction. Avoid gentle handshake, do not cross your arms or look away when speaking.

This may be a challenge if you are shy, but soon you will notice that you really feel better and more confident when you "rule" the room you are in.

2 Dress as a self-confident person

Every morning, as you prepare to leave the house, ask yourself: What would a confident person wear now? Then put on just that and watch your love for yourself grow. When you look better, you immediately feel better. Choosing clothes that look good to you, that are vibrant in color and appropriate to your personality will automatically increase your self-esteem.

Don't be afraid to let your personality get others attention. It is scientifically proven that clothes form a large part of the first impression on someone. Take advantage of this fact and shine as a confident person.

3 Speak wisely, clearly and loudly

Nothing gives off low self-esteem like a quiet and shy speech.

For this reason, speak only when you think and be wise. Use pause instead of whispers and stuttering. Just pause and give yourself a moment to think.

Speak firmly, but do not be aggressive and too loud. If you radiate confidence and know what you want to say, it will be much easier to hold the interviewee's attention than in a situation when you are shy and quiet. Therefore, your confidence will start to grow as people listen to the leader who radiates from you.

4 Think and act positively

Positive energy leads to positive outcomes. Therefore, train your mind to observe only the positive side of any situation, avoiding a negative attitude, which can make you feel less secure.

Smile, be cheerful and surround yourself with happy, positive people. There is nothing better for your confidence than the people with whom every activity is enjoyable and who enjoy your company.

As well as this attitude will help you really

make a difference in life in a different way, you will also start to see yourself differently. You will see your virtues much faster than your flaws, which will also add to your self-esteem.

5 Don't be afraid to take action

Obtaining confidence doesn't only mean working on your appearance and behavior, but also on your actions.

Be brave, courageous, innovative, creative and do something you otherwise wouldn't. Think like a person who has confidence. Practice this mindset and change the perspective from which you observe the challenges.

Each problem seems less important if you approach it with the idea that there is a solution, that is, that you are able to find a way out.

Most people feel they need to work on their weaknesses. A better idea for building confidence is to use your strength to the best of your ability.

Stop doubting your qualities. Believe in yourself and others will believe in you. It is the path to high self-esteem.

6 Be Organized

Nothing strengthens your confidence as an organization and preparedness for the situations that await you.

When you have a good organization, you also have better control over your time and responsibilities.

It is very important to be reliable and to plan your activities. It will bring you peace and self-respect when, after a hard day, you outline in your planner the obligations you have successfully completed.

7 Imagine yourself as a person you want to become

"Whatever the human mind can think and believe can be accomplished." - Napoleon Hill

Visualization is a technique of imagining what we want to become, what we want to be or what we want to have.

When we struggle with low self-esteem, usually that image of us first arises in our mind as a thought that we are not good enough. Then we believe in her and truly become a person of low self-esteem and self-confidence.

So now we can only correct this if we imagine ourselves as a person full of confidence, self-esteem and self-love. When you practice imagining a fantastic version of yourself, it will be much easier to believe in such a picture of yourself.

Once such a vision engages you in your mind, it will become a realistic image that you have of yourself.

8 Do something that scares you every day

The best way to overcome fear is to face it.

If you do at least one thing that scares you daily, over time, that experience will give you confidence, because you will realize that you are truly capable and courageous.

While this idea sounds incredibly scary, step out of the comfort zone and you will see most of your problems disappear before your eyes.

Take risks, be curious, try something new and allow yourself to be seen as a confident person. It is a great exercise for confidence, which can reveal you another, much nicer and more comfortable zone.

9 Accept your shortcomings and work on

yourself

We all have flaws and virtues, except that people full of confidence do not think that their flaws define them, but work on themselves until they become aware that they have many more virtues than flaws.

Learn and strive to be better, to gain knowledge and experience. Even if you fail in some intentions, it will be easier to endure failure if you do not consider it a definitive outcome and know that you are capable of reversing the situation and learning a lesson from it.

Get rid of perfectionism. Nobody is perfect.

So embrace the idea that everyone makes mistakes and you are allowed to so as well. Removing this kind of pressure will bring you confidence, as you will realize that no one is actually ideal, even though it may seem or appear so in your eyes.

10 Highlight your uniqueness

Each of us has some talent. We usually find it important only if it is amazing or if we excel at it.

However, every talent is important and you can use every one of them to boost your confidence. When you notice that you are good at something, you will immediately have a better opinion of yourself, especially if others notice your talent.

Accept yourself and your flaws, but highlight your virtues and talents.

If you have not yet recognized your talents, think about your hobbies and the things you enjoy doing in your spare time. You must have noticed people with talents that you didn't even know existed, so believe in yourself and your talents and get the best out of it.

Now that you know all these shortcuts to gain self-confidence and high self-esteem, work on looking at yourself differently. No one was born as the leader of a large company but worked to become one.

The success you think happened overnight actually started years before that.

Believe in yourself and your qualities, visualize success, be positive, be cheerful, act like a confident person and you will soon become that.

CONCLUSION

Once a person has gathered all of the facts there are to know about manipulation: who are manipulators, what are the techniques and signs of manipulation, how to prevent one's self from being manipulated, and how to gain confidence overall, the time has come to outsmart the master manipulator.

There are two points to remember when trying to outplay a manipulator. The first is being aware that one is in the presence of a manipulator and the second point is to actively look for opportunities to not be caught up in a manipulator's trap.

After a person knows that a manipulator is close by, there are steps that a person can take to keep the manipulator at arm's length. The first step is to avoid eye contact with the manipulator and if possible, ignore the manipulator all together. Manipulators feed off the observations they can decipher from the people around them. If a manipulator cannot pinpoint a person's strengths and weaknesses, they cannot exploit the person's flaws.

The second step is one that has been capitalized upon multiple times because it is a vital tool to prevent manipulation. Telling a manipulator "no" is a surefire way to stop a manipulator in their tracks. Their ability to control the people around them is contingent upon other people telling the manipulator "yes." It is important for people to remember that saying "no" does not make someone a bad person; it is healthy to take care of one's self instead of others once and a while.

Outsmarting a manipulator may also mean setting a person's own trap some of the time. One way to do so is to set goals and see whether or not someone tries to alter those goals to fit a new outcome. Manipulators try to influence people's desires to match their own and this trap allows for a person to see where the attempted influence begins. Additionally, having the goals mapped out already makes it more difficult for a manipulator to try to shift the focus of said goals.

The next step is to keep track of any written interaction one has with the manipulator. Do not overstep and invade their privacy by using any documentation that has not been obtained legally. For example, one cannot record a manipulator without their consent, but the text messages or email sent to you can be examined. There is also the option of keeping a journal that contains information about in-person meetings that have taken place. The paper trail and documentation of any interactions will force a manipulator to be held accountable for any wrongful doing. This is especially key for when a manipulator tries to place blame onto someone else.

It is also important to not become emotionally invested in a manipulator. This is easier said than done, but manipulators thrive on the emotional control they can gain over someone else. Once they learn what buttons to push and can question a person's mental capabilities, a manipulator can force someone to question their own mind, which leads to total dependency on a manipulator. If a person does not know if they can remain emotionally detached from a person, either chooses the option of ignoring the manipulator or refuse to make eye contact with them.

Providing a manipulator with the fear of the unknown is another great way to force a manipulator to question how to proceed. Manipulation is all about the ability to influence another person's thoughts and behaviors. However, if a person makes it particularly difficult to get what they want and it becomes too unpredictable to discover whether or not manipulation can eventually take place, the manipulator will cut their losses and move on to a new target.

Setting boundaries right off the bat is a way to make a manipulator aware that their antics will not be tolerated. Making statements such as "no you can't drive my car" or "no I want to hang out with my friends tonight" sets a tone that the manipulator is dealing with a confident and self-assertive individual.

Finally, be sure to hit a manipulator where it hurts. Manipulators typically have multiple people they are influencing at the same time, which opens up an opportunity to expose the manipulator's lies towards other people. Watch as one by one all of the manipulators allies turn against them until the manipulator are left with no one to control.

A manipulator is a person who takes control of another person in order to benefit them self in some way. Manipulators can be conniving but they can also be beneficial to others.

Manipulators can be sneaky, but they can also be exposed. Manipulation is a part of everyday life and how one uses their knowledge of manipulation is of their own free will.

What Did You Think of *Secretes of Manipulation, Persuasion and Suggestion?*

First of all, thank you for purchasing this book ***Secretes of Manipulation, Persuasion and Suggestion*** I know you could have picked any number of books to read, but you picked this book and for that I am extremely grateful.

I hope that it added at value and quality to your everyday life. If so, it would be really nice if you could share this book with your friends and family by posting to *Facebook* and *Twitter*.

If you enjoyed this book and found some benefit in reading this, I'd like to hear from you and hope that you could take some time to post a review on Amazon. Your feedback and support will help this author to greatly improve his writing craft for future projects and make this book even better. I want you, the reader, to know that your review is very important. I wish you all the best in your future success!